M000023361

CentOS System Administration Essentials

Become an efficient CentOS administrator by acquiring
real-world knowledge of system setup and configuration

Andrew Mallett

BIRMINGHAM - MUMBAI

CentOS System Administration Essentials

Copyright © 2014 Packt Publishing

All rights reserved. No part of this book may be reproduced, stored in a retrieval system, or transmitted in any form or by any means, without the prior written permission of the publisher, except in the case of brief quotations embedded in critical articles or reviews.

Every effort has been made in the preparation of this book to ensure the accuracy of the information presented. However, the information contained in this book is sold without warranty, either express or implied. Neither the author, nor Packt Publishing, and its dealers and distributors will be held liable for any damages caused or alleged to be caused directly or indirectly by this book.

Packt Publishing has endeavored to provide trademark information about all of the companies and products mentioned in this book by the appropriate use of capitals. However, Packt Publishing cannot guarantee the accuracy of this information.

First published: November 2014

Production reference: 1181114

Published by Packt Publishing Ltd.
Livery Place
35 Livery Street
Birmingham B3 2PB, UK.

ISBN 978-1-78398-592-0

www.packtpub.com

Cover image by Bartosz Chucherko (chucherko@gmx.com)

Credits

Author
Andrew Mallett

Reviewers
Jonathan Hobson

Manikandan Somasundaram

Ahmet Fuat Sungur

Commissioning Editor
Pramila Balan

Acquisition Editor
Richard Harvey

Content Development Editor
Akashdeep Kundu

Technical Editors
Vijin Boricha

Nikhil Potdukhe

Copy Editors
Merilyn Pereira

Adithi Shetty

Project Coordinator
Neha Thakur

Proofreaders
Paul Hindle

Clyde Jenkins

Indexer
Mariammal Chettiyar

Graphics
Sheetal Aute

Production Coordinator
Arvindkumar Gupta

Cover Work
Arvindkumar Gupta

About the Author

Andrew Mallett has worked in the IT field for more years than he cares to mention, well, since 1986, and with Linux technologies in Red Hat Linux 7 since 1999. Not only does he have Linux skills and certification, he consults and teaches Linux and other technologies and has had a book published with Packt Publishing on Citrix. He has also been an active participant in support communities, and works as a volunteer sysop on the SUSE Linux instructor to help, support, and develop the official Novell SUSE curriculum worldwide.

Andrew currently works for his own company and can be contacted at http://theurbanpenguin.com and @theurbanpenguin on Twitter. Video courses on Linux that he has published can be found at http://www.pluralsight.com.

I would like to thank Say Mistage (available on Twitter at @sayomgwtf) for keeping me sane with all of her doodles and inspiration during the writing of this book. Let me say that there are a few people in this world who suffer that never should. These people are often the most inspirational and happy people you find. Say is one of those people who suffers a lot in life but never lets it show.

About the Reviewers

Jonathan Hobson is a server engineer, developer, and database administrator who, for more than 20 years, has been working behind the scenes to support companies, organizations, and individuals around the world to realize their digital ambitions. As a keen exponent of Linux in the workplace (including RHEL, Fedora, Debian, Ubuntu, Mint, and many more), he has been using CentOS since its inception, and as the author of the best selling book *CentOS 6 Linux Server Cookbook*, *Packt Publishing*, he maintains a strong reputation for the generation of ideas, problem solving, building business confidence, and finding innovative solutions in challenging environments.

Beyond this, Jonathan enjoys writing code, publishing articles, listening to music, and walking his dogs in the great outdoors.

Manikandan Somasundaram has more than 3 years of experience in the field of Linux administration. He has a Bachelor of Engineering degree in Computer Science. Being a Linux enthusiast, he has specialized as a Red Hat Certified Engineer (RHCE) and Red Hat Certified Security Specialist (RHCSS). He is very interested in security implementation on servers. He started his career as a Systems Engineer in Linux in a small Chennai-based start-up company, where he had the freedom to explore/implement the world of open source. He migrated a number of software from proprietary to open source, such as the Openfire intranet chat server. He then moved to SafeScrypt, a business unit that is a part of Sify Technologies Limited, which is India's first certificate authority (CA), where he had an opportunity to work with the PKI infrastructure and certification practices. This helped him relate his RHCSS studies to reality. Currently, he is working for Mindtree Ltd. as a Linux system administrator and pursuing a Master's degree in Software Systems from BITS Pilani, India. His main hobby is to do freelance training on Linux administration. His other hobbies include yoga, martial arts, gymnastics, and playing the guitar.

He has previously reviewed *Implementing Samba 4*, *Packt Publishing*, and is happy that he got an opportunity to review this book as well.

I wish to thank the following people for inspiring me and contributing to my knowledge and helping me in reviewing this book:

I would like to thank my well-wishers: Prof. Vishvanathan, AVC College of Engineering, and Gerald Nathan, Principal Consultant at Corpus Software Private Limited. I would also like to thank my family: my father Somasundaram S., my mother Tamizarasi Somasundaram, and my sister Durgadevi Somasundaram.

Ahmet Fuat Sungur is an experienced computer engineer working with Global Maksimum Data and Information Technologies, a company that provides consultancy services on many products of Oracle (CEP, Coherence, database, DW, data mining), HP (Vertica), and Software AG (Apama and Terracotta).

He has around 8 years of IT experience working in the telecom and consultancy industries. He has worked on several products; they have changed over a period of time but the underlying OS has not. As an operating system engineer, he has worked especially on Oracle Enterprise Linux, Red Hat, and CentOS for several years.

Software architecture, distributed processing, Big Data, and columnar databases are his other main interests. He is also the reviewer of *Getting Started with Oracle Event Processing 11g, Packt Publishing*.

www.PacktPub.com

Support files, eBooks, discount offers, and more

For support files and downloads related to your book, please visit www.PacktPub.com.

Did you know that Packt offers eBook versions of every book published, with PDF and ePub files available? You can upgrade to the eBook version at www.PacktPub.com and as a print book customer, you are entitled to a discount on the eBook copy. Get in touch with us at service@packtpub.com for more details.

At www.PacktPub.com, you can also read a collection of free technical articles, sign up for a range of free newsletters and receive exclusive discounts and offers on Packt books and eBooks.

https://www2.packtpub.com/books/subscription/packtlib

Do you need instant solutions to your IT questions? PacktLib is Packt's online digital book library. Here, you can search, access, and read Packt's entire library of books.

Why subscribe?
- Fully searchable across every book published by Packt
- Copy and paste, print, and bookmark content
- On demand and accessible via a web browser

Free access for Packt account holders

If you have an account with Packt at www.PacktPub.com, you can use this to access PacktLib today and view 9 entirely free books. Simply use your login credentials for immediate access.

Table of Contents

Preface

Welcome to *CentOS System Administration Essentials*. My name is Andrew Mallett, and I will be offering you expert guidance and tuition, enabling you with the skills to tame this powerful and popular Linux distribution. I have chosen to write about CentOS primarily as it will not cost you to use it, neither while learning nor during production. Additionally, CentOS closely follows the Red Hat Enterprise Linux distribution, so the skills that you learn and develop here can be put to good use across both CentOS and Red Hat. Should you be interested, your reading can act as an investment in your career by pursuing the Red Hat certification paths. Although not directly written to fit into any existing curricula, the Red Hat exams are all based on practical exercises, so the more you know and understand about the operation of Linux, the better.

CentOS stands for Community Enterprise Operating System, and even though community is such a small word, it encompasses so much. The support emanates from the community, via fora and the Linux community, to help develop the services and applications, and provide remedies to bugs that occur. The community has taken ownership of this distribution. The distribution collectively becomes stronger with the continued involvement of a growing community.

While we talk of community, I would like to thank Say Mistage (available on Twitter at `@sayomgwtf`) for her inspiration and doodles.

Writing about an Enterprise Linux distribution is important as we see the increase in the number of organizations deploying Linux and, as a result, require knowledgeable professionals to manage these systems. In 2013, the Linux Foundation with Dice, a specialist recruitment company, surveyed many large organizations and found the following results:

- 93 percent of the organizations polled were looking to employ Linux professionals

- 91 percent of hiring managers reported that they found it difficult to find skilled Linux administrators

- As a side note to this, it was additionally noted that salaries for Linux professionals had increased by 9 percent during the previous 12 months

With such confidence in Linux within so many organizations, the focus of this book has to be commercially driven for both myself and you, the reader. I want you to be able to improve your career prospects as well as your Linux knowledge.

Enterprise Linux distributions such as CentOS, Red Hat, Debian, and SUSE Enterprise Linux generally do not deploy the latest and greatest bleeding edge technology that you might find in home or enthusiast-oriented distributions such as Fedora or openSUSE. Rather, they allow these to be development platforms to hone and perfect the software before migrating it to the enterprise platforms some months or even years later. Enterprise Linux has to be dependable, reliable, and resilient. On top of this, it must be well supported by both the organization deploying it, as well as the backend support coming from the community or paid support teams. The very latest in software development does not lend itself well to this by definition; as they are the most recent, the knowledge of these advancements, as well as their best practices, will without a doubt take time to evolve and develop.

What this book covers

Chapter 1, Taming vi, will make sure that you are fully versed in the shortcuts that exist to make your shell quickly navigable before entering into the realms of mastering vi. You may have some experience with vi but most often, I find that the experience has not been a good one. I am going to make sure that you are the master of vi and not vice versa.

Chapter 2, Cold Starts, is all about understanding the boot process in CentOS and learning how to not only modify the GRUB menu to make it more secure, but also how to use the GRUB command line to debug and repair boot issues. We will include a little boot splashing with Plymouth as well as explain when the root filesystem is not actually the root filesystem.

Chapter 3, CentOS Filesystems – A Deeper Look, tells us that we have files and directories but they are all just different file types. However, when it comes to links, pipes, and sockets, we will discuss what they are and how they are used. Regarding links, we will discuss what is the difference between a hard and soft link. Let's also challenge the traditional filesystem design; you may have worked with logical volumes manager (LVM) in the past, but let me tell you just how last century that is. You are going to be blown away by the power and ease of your enterprise filesystem management using BTRFS, pronounced as Better FS.

Chapter 4, YUM – Software Never Looked So Good, gets you to grips with YUM repositories and software management; you are going to love this. You will learn how to download packages without installing them, thus allowing you to easily distribute packages in your enterprise. If this is not good enough, then you'll learn how to set up a local repository to share packages across your LAN and create your own RPMs.

Chapter 5, Herding Cats – Taking Control of Processes, tells us that too often, administrators, without the insight that you and I have, will leave services running that aren't required, and do not understand the tools they have to manage processes. You will learn here to control services and processes using upstart and traditional service scripts as well as become homicidal with the kill and pkill weapons of choice.

Chapter 6, Users – Do We Really Want Them?, tells us, of course, that we do not want them (users) on our system, but it is often dictated, so we have little choice. Rather than be grumpy about this, you will learn how to manage users with a smile and keep them on a tight rein.

Chapter 7, LDAP – A Better Type of User, tells us that rather than having silos of users and groups on each machine, it is better to get back on the golf course by spending more time improving the system and less time managing users. Adding users to a central directory and sharing them across all systems as required is your gateway to freedom.

Chapter 8, Nginx – Deploying a Performance-centric Web Server, tells us that commonly, Linux administrators and publications concentrate on the Apache web server; I will introduce you to the new kid on the block, Nginx (pronounced Engine X). Introduced in 2004, Nginx is rapidly taking market share from Apache and has already surpassed IIS in a number of deployed web servers worldwide. We will deploy Nginx and PHP.

Chapter 9, Puppet – Now You Are the Puppet Master, shifts our focus from Linux in the enterprise to taking control of your enterprise systems with the renowned Puppet software from Puppet Labs. Central configuration control is as good as centralized user management in giving you more time to spend on the golf course, not that I want you to think that golf dominates my life.

Chapter 10, Security Central, introduces you to Pluggable Authentication Modules (PAM). It is your friend and will help you manage when and how users connect. SELinux, again, is a friend, albeit a temperamental one. When treated well, it will help you ensure correct use of your system. You will learn how to harden your Linux system and gain a set of best practices!

Chapter 11, Graduation Day, tells us that as we prepare to leave with our newfound skills, we will remind ourselves the need for security and adhere to the best practices. We can revisit some of the products that we have seen before, such as Puppet and Nginx, and outline some industry-recognized guidelines for the deployment of these services, along with some of the new features of CentOS 7.

What you need for this book

You will be expected to have knowledge about working with Linux and look to fast-track that knowledge to an expert level. Working along with this book and the exercises therein is recommended and encouraged. Although this book can be used as a "read and learn", I would recommend "read, try, and learn for life". The try bit in the middle is essential to any real understanding and knowledge; this is a pedagogy that has been tried and tested across ages.

At the time of writing this book, CentOS version 6.5 is released, although any version of CentOS is acceptable for most of the exercises, including later versions. Versions of CentOS can be downloaded from http://wiki.centos.org/Download. It is free and open to use, as you will see, under the terms of the GPL license. CentOS 6.5 supports updates free of charge up to November 30, 2020.

Who this book is for

I think it is fair to say that I know Linux, and more importantly, how to keep you engaged. I will deliver my knowledge to you in a way that is designed to help you understand and remember, by breaking down complex ideas into easy-to-consume nuggets of wisdom, enabling you to grow in knowledge and confidence with the turn of every page. We will concentrate on the power and ease of use of the command line. For instance, let me ask you this question:

What was the date 73 days ago?

I am surprised that you do not know. The Linux command line knows, simply by executing the following command:

```
$ date --date "73 days ago"
```

This book has been written to target those Linux administrators with some level of knowledge and who wish to gain further experience and are not frightened of getting their hands dirty using the command-line shell.

Understanding the power of the Linux command line and being able to master it with little enhancements like these will be your key to success as a Linux administrator. This is where I will differentiate this book from others that you may see. You may also want to view my YouTube channel at http://www.youtube.com/theurbanpenguin, where I have created over 700 tutorials on various products that interest mostly Linux with a lot of scripting and programming too.

Alternatively, you can visit my own site at http://theurbanpenguin.com, where the content is better organized.

Conventions

In this book, you will find a number of text styles that distinguish among different kinds of information. Here are some examples of these styles and an explanation of their meaning.

Code words in text, database table names, folder names, filenames, file extensions, pathnames, dummy URLs, user input, and Twitter handles are shown as follows: "Getting the .vimrc setup the way you like."

A block of code is set as follows:

```
default=0
timeout=5
hiddenmenu
password --md5 <password-hash>
```

Any command-line input or output is written as follows:

```
# vi /etc/httpd/conf/httpd.conf
# service httpd restart
w3m localhost
```

New terms and **important words** are shown in bold. Words that you see on the screen, for example, in menus or dialog boxes, appear in the text like this: "From the main welcome page, we should choose the **Users and Groups** tab and then select the **Search** button."

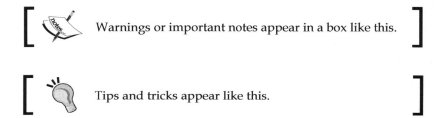

Warnings or important notes appear in a box like this.

Tips and tricks appear like this.

Reader feedback

Feedback from our readers is always welcome. Let us know what you think about this book—what you liked or disliked. Reader feedback is important for us as it helps us develop titles that you will really get the most out of.

To send us general feedback, simply e-mail feedback@packtpub.com, and mention the book's title in the subject of your message.

If there is a topic that you have expertise in and you are interested in either writing or contributing to a book, see our author guide at www.packtpub.com/authors.

Customer support

Now that you are the proud owner of a Packt book, we have a number of things to help you to get the most from your purchase.

Downloading the color images of this book

We also provide you with a PDF file that has color images of the screenshots/diagrams used in this book. The color images will help you better understand the changes in the output. You can download this file from: `https://www.packtpub.com/sites/default/files/downloads/5920OS_coloredimages.pdf`.

Errata

Although we have taken every care to ensure the accuracy of our content, mistakes do happen. If you find a mistake in one of our books—maybe a mistake in the text or the code—we would be grateful if you could report this to us. By doing so, you can save other readers from frustration and help us improve subsequent versions of this book. If you find any errata, please report them by visiting `http://www.packtpub.com/submit-errata`, selecting your book, clicking on the **Errata Submission Form** link, and entering the details of your errata. Once your errata are verified, your submission will be accepted and the errata will be uploaded to our website or added to any list of existing errata under the Errata section of that title.

To view the previously submitted errata, go to `https://www.packtpub.com/books/content/support` and enter the name of the book in the search field. The required information will appear under the **Errata** section.

Piracy

Piracy of copyrighted material on the Internet is an ongoing problem across all media. At Packt, we take the protection of our copyright and licenses very seriously. If you come across any illegal copies of our works in any form on the Internet, please provide us with the location address or website name immediately so that we can pursue a remedy.

Please contact us at `copyright@packtpub.com` with a link to the suspected pirated material.

We appreciate your help in protecting our authors and our ability to bring you valuable content.

Questions

If you have a problem with any aspect of this book, you can contact us at `questions@packtpub.com`, and we will do our best to address the problem.

1
Taming vi

You may have some experience with vi, or what is now known as Vim (which is when simply put—vi improved). All too often, I find that those first experiences have never been good ones or to be looked back upon with much fondness. Guiding you through the initially unfathomable regime of vi, we are going to make sure that you are the master of vi and you leave wanting to use this tool from the gods. vi is like everything else in the sense that you just need to stick with it in the early days and keep practicing. Remember how you persevered for many hours riding your bicycle as a toddler and became a master, despite a few bruised knees? I want you to persevere with vi too. We will start with a little command-line magic to make the whole **command-line interface (CLI)** experience a better one. We will then be ready to start our black-belt experience in vi.

In this chapter, we will go through the following topics:

- **CLI trickery** – shortcuts that you will love

- **Vim and vi**: In this section, you will learn to differentiate between these twins and meet their graphical cousin

- **Getting the .vimrc setup the way you like**

- **Search and replace**: In this section, you will learn how to quickly find and replace text within files from both inside and outside Vim

- **Learning to remove extraneous comments from a file with a few deft key strokes**

CLI trickery – shortcuts that you will love

So before we dice into the wonderful world of text editing that is vi, we will warm up with a few exercises on the keyboard. Linux is my passion, as is automation. I am always keen to create scripts to carry out tasks so that those tasks become repeatedly correct. Once the script is created and tested, we will have the knowledge and faith that it will run in the same way every time and we will not make mistakes or miss critical steps, either because it gets boring or we are working late on a Friday night and just want to go home. Scripting itself is just knowing the command line well and being able to use it at its best. This truth remains across all systems that you will work with.

On the command line, we may try a little more black magic by executing the following command:

```
$ cd dir1 || mkdir dir1 && cd dir1
```

With this, we have used the cd command to enter the dir1 directory. The double pipe or vertical bar indicates that we will attempt the next command only if the first command fails. This means that if we fail to switch to the dir1 directory, we will run the mkdir dir1 command to create it. If the directory creation succeeds, we then change into that directory.

 The || part denotes that the second command will run only on the failure of the first. The && part denotes that the second command will run only if the first command succeeds.

The command history is a little more and hugely better than just an up arrow key! Consider the following commands:

```
$ mkdir dir1
$ cd !$
```

The !$ part represents the last argument, so in this way, the second line evaluates to the following:

```
$ cd dir1
```

In this way, we can rewrite the initial command sequence, by combining both concepts, to create the following command:

```
$ cd dir1 || mkdir !$ && cd !$
```

We can repeat the last command as well as the last argument. More importantly, we can specify the start characters for the last command. If it was merely the last command, then the up arrow key would suffice. If we were working on a web server configuration, we may want to edit the configuration file with vi, start the service, and then test with a command-line browser. We can represent these tasks using the following three commands:

```
# vi /etc/httpd/conf/httpd.conf

# service httpd restart

w3m localhost
```

Having run these three commands in the correct order, hoping for success, we may notice that we still have issues and that we need to start re-editing the configuration file for Apache, the web server. We can now abbreviate the command list to the following:

```
# !v

# !s

# !w
```

The !v command will rerun the last command in my history that begins with a v, and likewise with s and w. This way, we can appear to be terribly proficient and working really quickly, thus gaining more time to do what really interests us, perhaps a short 9 holes?

In a similar fashion to our first glance at the history using the !$ symbols to represent the last argument, we can use !?73. This would look for 73 anywhere as an argument or part of an argument. With my current history, this would relate to the date command we ran earlier. Let's take a look:

```
$ !?73
```

With my history, the sequence will expand to and run the following command:

```
$ date --date "73 days ago"
```

Looking at my command history from the last command run to the first, we search for 73 anywhere as a command argument. We make a note that we exclusively look for 73, meaning we are looking for the character 7 followed by the character 3. We have to then bear in mind that we would also match 273 or 733 if they existed in my history.

Having mastered a little of the Bash shell history functions, we should practice to make this second nature.

Vim and vi

Ah yes, Vim and vi! They sound like some ancient mystic potion that ensures long life and wisdom. Alas though, they are not.

The command-line text editor vi was first written in 1976 and became part of the first release of BSD Unix in 1978. Even though it is command line driven and with no **Graphical User Interface (GUI)** or menu, a 2009 survey conducted by Linux Journal found that vi was the most popular editor, beating even gedit, the GUI GNOME editor, into second place. I am not averse to the GUI, but I find a GUI editor to be restrictive and slow. I can honestly say that the majority of, if not all, tasks can be performed by me more quickly in vi.

That being said, in CentOS, you will not find vi; vi is purely a default alias that is provided for convenience, and links to the `vim` command. We can view this on my CentOS 6.5 console using the following command:

```
$ alias | grep vi
```

The output of the command should look similar to the following screenshot:

```
[andrew@centos ~]$ alias | grep vi
alias vi='vim'
[andrew@centos ~]$ █
```

Vim is a contraction of **Vi IMproved** and was first publicly released in 1991 and authored by Bram Moolenaar, initially targeted at the Amiga system. It has been common in the Linux platform since the early 2000s. As the name suggests, it is based on vi and is improved; on CentOS, it is distributed with the `vim-enhanced` package. These improvements are most commonly useful with the syntax-highlighting feature available for languages such as PERL, Python, and PHP. Another such improvement is that it can work traditionally on the command line or with a GUI frontend. To install the graphical interface for Vim, you will need to add the `vim-X11` package as follows:

```
# yum install -y vim-X11
```

One limitation, of course, is that you will require the X11 server to be running. In an enterprise, the server will often run without a GUI and you can connect using secure shell to a command-line shell only.

If you are new to vi, then using the graphical version can be helpful, as the menus also display the command-line shortcuts. To edit a file with vi or Vim on the command line, we can simply use a command similar to the following:

```
$ vi <filename-to-edit>
```

It is possible to use the graphical version of an editor when you are working on the CentOS desktop as follows:

```
$ gvim <filename-to-edit>
```

or

```
$ vimx -g <filename-to-edit>
```

I would recommend using the `gvim` command, as it doesn't require the additional option and causes less confusion. Starting `vimx` without the `-g` option just starts the normal Vim program.

Getting the .vimrc setup the way you like

As with many programs in Linux, Vim has the option to read settings from a run-control file. This can be centralized via the `/etc/vimrc` file, or for each user via the `~/.vimrc` file. With this file, especially with our own version, you can customize how Vim appears and controls its functionalities.

Firstly, we will look at line numbering. Often when we edit a file, we do so as the console has reported an error on a particular line just after we have tried running a script or starting a service; we know we have a syntax error. Let's say we want to go directly to the offending line 97 of the `test.php` file. Then, we would duly type:

```
$ vi +97 test.php
```

This is assuming that we were in the same directory as our file. Similarly, should we want to go directly to the first occurrence of the word `install` within the `readme` file, we could issue the following command:

```
$ vi +/install readme
```

Then, as if by magic, we are transported to the correct line that we require. However, in the case of the word `search`, the word that was `search` is highlighted in color. If that is not desirable, then we can simply turn off that feature. Within Vim, we can type:

```
:nohlsearch
```

If there are settings that we want to make permanent within Vim, we can edit the
`.vimrc` file in our home directory. This is our own personal settings file and as such,
changes made here will not affect anyone else. If we want to affect system-wide
settings, then we can use the `/etc/vimrc` file. Try adding the following line to the
`~/.vimrc` file to persistently disable the highlight `search`:

```
set nohlsearch
```

With this addition, each time we start Vim, the setting is ready for us. As we view
our files though, from within Vim, we may prefer to have line numbering turned
on. Sometimes this makes life easier, but other times, we may prefer to have line
numbering off, especially in cases where we have lines starting with numbers
(because the display can become confusing). To enable line numbering, run the
following command:

```
:set number
```

To turn line numbering off, we can use the following command:

```
:set nonumber
```

As before, we can always put the desired start-up value in the `.vimrc` file. However,
before we do this, let's look at key mappings within Vim and how we can create a
shortcut to toggle line numbering on and off. We would like to create a mapping
for the normal mode in Vim. This is the mode when we first enter Vim and we are
not editing, just navigating the file; using the *Esc* key, we can always return to the
normal mode. Execute the following command:

```
:nmap <C-N> : set invnumber<CR>
```

The `nmap` command denotes that we are making a mapping for the normal mode
only. We are mapping the *Ctrl* + *N* keys to run the sub command `:set invnumber`
followed by `<CR>`.

With this in place, we can now use the combination of *Ctrl* + *N* to toggle line
numbering on and off. Now we are really starting to make some steam with this
product, and you can gain some appreciation of why it is so popular. Before we
make the final edit to the `.vimrc` file, we will see how to navigate lines by number
while in vi or Vim. Making sure that we are in the normal mode using the *Esc* key,
we can use `2G` or `2gg` to navigate to line 2 of the current file; likewise, `234G` or `234gg`
would go to line 234 and `G` or `gg` would navigate to the end of the file. Simple but
not simple enough; I would prefer to type the line number followed by the *Enter*
key. For this, we map the *Enter* key to `G`. If we choose to use the *Enter* key without a
preceding number, then we are taken directly to the end of the document, just as we
would is we used the key `G` by itself. Execute the following command:

```
:nmap <CR> G
```

Now we simply type in the desired line number followed by *Enter*. This in turn is interpreted as the number followed by *G*. In this way, we can navigate easily to the correct line. We can persist this setting by adding the following text to the `.vimrc` file, which should now read similar to the following text as we review all the settings made within this subsection:

```
set nohlsearch number
nmap <C-N> : set invnumber<CR>
nmap <CR> G
```

Now sit back and enjoy what you have achieved, remembering though that practice is the key to knowledge being retained.

Search and replace

So we are not exactly on a "search and destroy" mission, but if it helps by adding a little enjoyment to our learning, then we can embark upon a search and replace mission. Linux has a huge amount of power available on the command line and nothing less than the stream editor, sed. Even without entering the Vim editor, we can search for and replace text in a single file or even across multiple files. Not having to use an interactive editor opens up more administrative scope to us by being able to script updates across a single or many servers. The functionality we have in the `sed` command is available to us for use from within Vim or as a standalone application. We will be learning in this subsection how to search for and replace text within files using sed and from within Vim, building skills that we can use across CentOS and other operating systems including OS X on the Mac.

Firstly, let's take a scenario that we have recently changed our company name and we need to change all the references of `Dungeons` in a text document to `Dragons`. Using sed, we could run the command directly from the console:

```
$ sed -i 's/Dungeons/Dragons/g' /path/file
```

This will read the file line by line, replacing all occurrences of the string `Dungeons` with `Dragons`. The `-i` option allows for in-pace edits, meaning we edit the file without the need to redirect the output from sed to a new file. The `g` option allows for the replacement to occur across all instances of `Dragon` even if it appears more than once per line.

To do the same within Vim where we have the file open, run the following command:

```
:%s/Dungeons/Dragons/g
```

The percent symbol is used to specify the range as the whole document; whereas if we use the following command, we would only search lines 3 through 12 inclusive of the search string. In this case, the range is said to be lines 3 to 12 whereas with %, the range is the complete document.

```
:3,12s/Dungeons/Dragons/g
```

The range can be very useful when perhaps we want to indent some code in a file. In the following line, we again search lines 3 through to 12 and add a Tab to the start of each line:

```
:s/3,12s/^/\t/
```

We have set the range in the previous command within Vim to represent lines 3 to 12 again. These lines may represent the contents of an `if` statement, for example, that we would like to indent. We search first for the carat symbol, ^ (the start of a line), and replace it with a tab (\t). There is no need for the global option as the start of a line obviously only occurs once per line. Using this method, we can quickly add indents to a file as required, and we are again Zen superheroes of Vim.

Learning to remove extraneous comments from a file with a few deft key strokes

Now that we are the administrator, the Zen master of search and replace, we can use these skills to tidy configuration files that often have many hundreds of commented lines within them. I do not mind documentation but when it becomes such an overwhelming majority, it can take over. Consider the `httpd.conf` Apache configuration file under `/etc/httpd/conf/`. This has 675 commented lines. We perhaps want to keep the original file as a reference. So let's first make a copy by executing the following command; we know how to do this from the *Preface* of this book and if you did not read it, now is your chance to read it before a letter goes home to your parents.

```
# cd /etc/httpd/conf
# cp httpd.conf    httpd.conf.$(date +%F)
```

We can easily list the commented lines using the following command that counts the lines that begin with the # sign, a comment:

```
# egrep -c '^#' httpd.conf
```

On my system, we see that there are 675 such lines. Using sed or Vim, we can remove the comments, firstly, with sed, as follows:

```
# sed  -i '/^#/d' httpd.conf
```

Then, within Vim with the file open, it is a little different:

```
:g/^#/d
```

The result is the same in both examples where we have reduced the numbers of lines in the file by about two-thirds.

Summary

In each chapter, I want to make sure that there has been at least one item of value that you feel you can take away with you and use; how did I do in this chapter? If you recall, we have reviewed a few shortcuts that may help us navigate the command history effectively. Quickly, we moved on to discover the text editor vi or, more commonly now, Vim. For those that need a little help getting started with Vim, we additionally have gVim available to use if we are working on the desktop. Customizing any system is important to make us feel that we own the system and it works for us. With Vim, we can use the .vimrc file found in our home directory. We were able to add a little bling to Vim with some extra key mapping and desirable options. From then on, it was straight down to work to see what Vim could do, and how the search and replace and delete options that we reviewed worked.

2
Cold Starts

In the Northern Hemisphere, I think we can all relate to the analogy of the cold start; those bleak January mornings where you are frantically trying to start your car. When it does finally splutter into some form of life, we then have to contend with a steering wheel too cold to hold. Thankfully, starting up a Linux system is not so unpleasant; perhaps air-conditioned server rooms have something to do with this, I am not sure…

Working through this chapter, we are going to build upon what you have already mastered—helping you understand your Linux systems. You will learn about the following topics:

- **The GRUB and the MBR**: In this section, you will learn about the relationship that the **GRand Unified Bootloader (GRUB)** enjoys with the **Master Boot Record (MBR)**, being able to slip its slender 466 bytes easily inside the 512-byte limit.

- **When is the root filesystem not the root filesystem?**: In this section, we will understand the term *root* when used as a directive within a GRUB stanza, which is a little hurdle we shall overcome.

- **Working on the GRUB console**: In this section, you will learn how to enable some powerful recovery tools.

- **Protecting the GRUB menu with passwords**: In this section, you will learn how to enforce physical security of your systems: desktops or servers.

- **Boot splashing with plymouth**: A little fun to finish the section with, we will look at the range of boot splash screens that we can use with CentOS. By the end of this chapter, your Linux system will never have been so well dressed.

The GRUB and MBR

This is not just a competition to see how many acronyms we can fit into a chapter heading, although, out of four words, having used two already is not a bad start. The **GRUB** is the system-supplied bootloader that ships with CentOS and Red Hat Enterprise Linux 6. This tiny piece of bootstrap code is used to load the kernel and allows us to dual boot different Linux versions or even with Microsoft Windows operating systems. The GRUB has been the bootloader of choice for many years, although other bootloaders do exist. These include:

- **Lilo**: This is the original Linux loader
- **EXTLinux**: This is part of the SYSLinux family that includes the following:
    - EXTLinux to boot from fixed drives
    - ISOLinux to boot from CDs and DVDs
    - SYSLinux to boot from a USB device
    - PXELinux to boot from the network
- **GRUB2**: More recently, this is making its appearance as a replacement to GRUB, or what is now referred to as the legacy GRUB. GRUB2 is likely to debut in CentOS 7 in 2014.

The GRUB bootloader is most commonly stored in the MBR of the bootable drive.

 Although generally stored within the MBR, it is possible to install GRUB into the superblock, or the first 512 bytes, of a partition.

The MBR makes up the first 512 bytes of the disk, allowing up to 466 bytes of storage for the bootloader; the additional space will be used to store the partition table for that drive.

We can back up the MBR to a file using the dd command as follows:

```
# dd if=/dev/sda of=/tmp/sda.mbr count=1 bs=512
```

The dd command is used to duplicate a disk. In the previous command, we read from the first disk, /dev/sda, and backed it up to the /tmp/sda.mbr file. Rather than duplicating the entire disk, we limit the backup to a count of one block of 512 bytes.

Now that we have a backup for the MBR, we can investigate this fact a little more by running the following command:

 The following commands can be destructive, in that they will destroy the MBR, so please take care if you will be running commands on your own system, and I would recommend running only the following demonstration commands on a test system.

```
# dd if=/dev/zero of=/dev/sda count=1 bs=512
```

With the preceding command, we have wiped the data stored within the first 512 bytes of the disk /dev/sda. The MBR now is effectively cleared. We can verify this by using the following command:

```
$ lsblk /dev/sda
```

The output should display an empty partition table. The system remains usable as the partition table is resident to the RAM on the running system; however, until we are able to restore the MBR, a reboot will soon identify how much of a disaster we are in. Never fear, we can restore the MBR from the backup. What dd takes away, dd can return, simply by using the dd command as follows. Quickly, before someone notices!

```
# dd if=/tmp/sda.mbr of=/dev/sda
```

We do not need to limit the amount of data to be read from the specified file. Remember, it only contains the 512 bytes that make up the MBR. With a little luck, using the fdisk command will now show the partition table correctly as it was before, and you can begin to breathe easy again:

```
$ fdisk /dev/sda
```

 Using the dd command to wipe a disk completely with the /dev/zero input file is useful should you wish to wipe a disk before selling a computer, ensuring that the operating system, applications, and most importantly, the data is not sold with the device. We use fdisk in the second example as lsblk reads from memory and not the disk.

Once we have booted into GRUB, a menu will be shown allowing the user to select the **operating system (OS)** to enter. In general, the default selection is loaded without user interaction. We can configure the menu choices using the /boot/grub/menu.1st file. You will learn more about this file later.

When is the root filesystem not the root filesystem?

We now need to break down the menu entries within the file, identifying the core components so that we can understand how they relate to the system and, most importantly, how we can correct errors.

Editing stanzas in GRUB

Each entry in the GRUB menu is known as a **stanza**, and each stanza will start with the `title` word, containing three directives as follows:

- `root`
- `kernel`
- `initd`

The title of the stanza also becomes the displayed item in the menu. Let's consider a stanza that begins with the following title:

```
title CentOS 6.5 OS
```

The menu will display `CentOS 6.5 OS` as the selectable item, and it is important to note that we do not add quotes around the text as they will also be displayed to the user. This is unless, of course, you want or need to display these quotes; we are most certainly not quote unfriendly at Packt Publishing!

Adding a root entry to a stanza

Directly following the stanza title will be a line that starts with the `root` directive. This identifies the root filesystem to GRUB and not the OS root; in simple terms, this should point to the partition that is marked as bootable in the partition table.

We can use the `fdisk` or `parted` command to display the bootable partition. If you are using the `fdisk` command to display the partition information, the command would be similar to the following where we want to list the partitions of the first hard drive within the system:

```
# fdisk -l /dev/sda
```

The partition marked as bootable will be identified with an asterisk mark. If you are using the `parted` command to display the partition table, you will be able to identify the bootable partition by the boot flag by executing the following command:

```
# parted /dev/sda print
```

The `fdisk` shows the bootable partition with * and parted with the word `boot`.

The bootable partition can be `/boot` or the actual root filesystem itself `/`. This relates to how the system was configured as it was installed. It might often be the case that `/boot` will have its own partition to ease access by the bootloader. The legacy GRUB, for example, cannot access a filesystem built on **Logical Volume Management (LVM)**; this is the default partitioning proposal in CentOS 6. The same applies to software **Redundant Array of Inexpensive Disks (RAID)** arrays.

Consider the following stanza:

```
title CentOS 6.5 OS
   root (hd0,0)
```

From this, we can determine that GRUB should mount the first partition on the first drive (both the drive and partition numbering starts at 0) as the bootable partition.

To summarize, the `root` directive in a GRUB stanza indicates the partition that the MBR marks as bootable.

Adding a kernel entry to a stanza

The directive, `kernel`, directs the bootloader to the target operating system kernel. The path to that kernel will be related to the GRUB root partition, or the bootable partition. If the path reads `/vmlinuz.version`, then this would be an indication that the kernel is located at the root of the bootable partition, whereas the path `/boot/vmlinuz.version` would indicate that the bootable partition is the Linux or OS root partition. The path has to include the `/boot` directory to be able to locate the kernel.

Following the filename of the kernel are the arguments used when loading the kernel, or more simply referred to as the kernel options. These options include, among others, the device name where the real root filesystem is located and the device name for the swap filesystem, which can be used to suspend the system, perhaps on a laptop build. An example of the OS root option would be `root=/dev/sda2`; this being the second partition on the first hard drive or `root=/dev/mapper/vg_centos-vg_root`. This indicates that the operating system root is built upon an LVM. The swap filesystem to be suspended is indicated by the `resume` option.

The following extract from a stanza indicates that the boot partition is /dev/sda1 (hd0,0) and the operating system root is /dev/sda2, with the swap located on /dev/sda3:

```
title CentOS 6.5 OS
  root (hd0,0)
  kernel /vmlinuz.version root=/dev/sda2 resume=/dev/sda3
```

If the OS root is also the bootable partition, the corresponding GRUB stanza would read similar to the following:

```
title CentOS 6.5 OS
  root (hd0,0)
  kernel /boot/vmlinuz.version root=/dev/sda1 resume=/dev/sda2
```

We can see that the path to the kernel is now the full operating system path and both the GRUB root and the OS root correspond to the same partition.

Given a running system where the boot process is completed and we are logged in, it is possible to view the version of the kernel with either of the following commands:

- $ cat /proc/version
- $ uname -r

You should look at both commands and see which one best suits your needs; the /proc/version file will give a little more information. However, the uname -r command summarizes the information well. This is your system and it is your choice.

Should we need to list the options with which the kernel was booted, we can display those options with the following command:

$ cat /proc/cmdline

By this stage, I am hoping you have a little more understanding of when the root filesystem may not actually be the root filesystem and when it can be the root filesystem. You are now ready to use this riddle anytime that you wish to confuse your colleagues. It really is a simple matter of knowing where the partition that holds the kernel is; this then becomes the root of the bootable partition. The OS root is what we normally think as of the root filesystem but this happens only once the system has completed the boot process. The kernel directive simply points to the kernel file with a path relative to the root of the boot partition along with any options that we may wish to pass through to the kernel when it is loaded.

The /proc directory is a pseudo filesystem, meaning that it is transient and resides only in the RAM. It contains up-to-date information for the currently running system. This directory is worth becoming acquainted with.

Adding an initrd entry to a stanza

Similar to the kernel directive, the initrd directive will point to the initialization RAM disk; a mini OS that is compiled with the drivers needed to access the OS root filesystem. The RAM disk loads prior to the kernel and mounts the OS root filesystem as read-only. Filesystem integrity checks are performed before handing it to the kernel to continue with the boot process and mounting as read/write. This means that the kernel does not have to have the drivers for the root filesystem internally compiled, allowing more flexibility in changes to the OS root and a more lean kernel. The RAM disk can be recompiled if the root filesystem changes or the drivers need to access the hardware change with the mkinitrd command.

Continuing with our example stanza, we can insert a line for the initrd directive to read as follows:

```
title CentOS 6.5 OS
   root (hd0,0)
   kernel /boot/vmlinuz.version root=/dev/sda1 resume=/dev/sda2
   initrd /boot/initramfs.version
```

Not wishing to be out performed by the preceding simple text, the following screenshot shows an extract from a real GRUB stanza on my CentOS 6.5 system.

```
title CentOS (2.6.32-431.el6.x86_64)
        root (hd0,0)
        kernel /vmlinuz-2.6.32-431.el6.x86_64 ro root=/dev/mapper/vg_centos65-lv
_root rd_NO_LUKS  KEYBOARDTYPE=pc KEYTABLE=uk LANG=en_US.UTF-8 rd_NO_MD rd_LVM_L
V=vg_centos65/lv_swap SYSFONT=latarcyrheb-sun16 crashkernel=auto rd_LVM_LV=vg_ce
ntos65/lv_root rd_NO_DM rhgb quiet vga=0x340
        initrd /initramfs-2.6.32-431.el6.x86_64.img
```

Working on the GRUB console

When presented with the GRUB menu, as well as selecting the entry we wish to boot, we can either edit existing entries or shell out to the GRUB console. Working on the GRUB console enables us to enter our own sets of commands. Remember the trilogy that should accompany each stanza:

- root
- kernel
- initrd

We can enter these commands, but also reinstall GRUB if required. More simply, in the console, we can also edit or append to the exiting entries; using the *e* key, we can edit an entry, and *a* can be used to append an option to the kernel line. From the following screenshot, we can view these options:

```
Use the ↑ and ↓ keys to select which entry is highlighted.
Press enter to boot the selected OS, 'e' to edit the
commands before booting, 'a' to modify the kernel arguments
before booting, or 'c' for a command-line.
```

Editing the kernel arguments allows you to specify the runlevel target to boot to; using this method, it is possible to reset the password of the root user.

To recover a forgotten root password, we can boot the system to runlevel 1; by default, this will log you in directly as root.

1. Firstly, we must select the entry in the menu to boot to. If there is more than one, do not use the *Enter* key.

2. With the menu entry highlighted, choose the letter *a*.

3. This will take you directly to the end of the kernel line where you can add the number 1 to boot to runlevel 1.

 It is important to note that *CentOS System Administration Essentials* assumes that no prior runlevel has already been specified in the kernel arguments.

With the number added, just hit the *Enter* key, and the system will boot to the single user mode and logged in as root. Once the system has been booted, you can effectively change a password using the `passwd` command.

It is possible to prevent this behavior; we have to be cautious to avoiding the prevention genuine recovery mechanisms of our server. If there is enough physical protection of the server, then perhaps we do not need to make any changes. However, if we cannot ensure physical security of the server, we can edit the `/etc/sysconfig/init` file by changing the `SINGLE=/sbin/sushell` line to the following:

```
SINGLE=/sbin/sulogin
```

The `sulogin` command will prompt for the root user's password.

 If `sulogin` has been set and you still need emergency access as root, it is possible by specifying `init=/bin/bash` instead of 1 as the runlevel.

If our boot situation is a little more serious, or in human terms, it won't boot, then we can enter the GRUB command prompt using the option `c`. Using the command `help`, we can determine what commands are available from the minimal shell. To reinstall GRUB with the correct drivers to access the boot partition, execute the following command:

```
grub> setup(hd0)
```

The preceding command will check to see if `/boot/grub/stage1` or `/grub/stage1` exists on the bootable partition. This way, it determines which partition to use as root and copies the `stage1` file to the MBR complete with the drivers needed to access the bootable partition. We can then choose to restart the system with the `reboot` command.

Not only can we use the GRUB console to repair GRUB, we can use it to boot the system and verify the menu items. By specifying the root filesystem to be used for booting, we can check the path required to access the kernel and `initrd`. We can use the normal tab completion on the GRUB shell to see directories and filenames.

Protecting the GRUB menu with passwords

Now I can imagine that all of this talk to gain root access from the physical server can be quite alarming; the truth is that it really shouldn't be, as securing physical access to the server is normally not difficult or onerous. However, where there is a desire or need to take the security further, it can easily be implemented through GRUB passwords. Any password settings will normally be added to the global section that precedes any stanza. Firstly, let's review some of the GRUB global options before setting some passwords.

On visiting the `/boot/grub/menu.1st` file on CentOS, we will see that the first lines are commented out and generated by the installer **anaconda**, and that the file is named as `grub.conf`.

The `menu.1st` file does exist in Red Hat and CentOS but is in the guise of a symbolic link to `/boot/grub/grub.conf`. From the legacy GRUB documentation, the file should be `menu.1st`; CentOS provides this with the link, but I feel that the file is more logically named `grub.conf`.

For ease of access, a symbolic link `/etc/grub.conf` links through the `/boot/grub/grub.conf` file. The single file can then be accessed as follows:

```
/boot/grub/grub.conf
/boot/grub/menu.1st
/etc/grub.conf
```

The `default` directive will direct GRUB to the default stanza or entry if no choice is made before the timeout.

```
default=0
timeout=5
hiddenmenu
```

Here, we will select the first stanza, stanza 0, if no selection has been made within 5 seconds of the menu loading. The directive, `hiddenmenu`, prevents the menu from showing unless the *Esc* key is pressed. This is especially helpful where there is only one entry in the menu, which is often the case, making good and practical sense.

If you need to prevent users from selecting anything other than what is provided via the menu, then we can add a password to the global settings. This will ensure that, unless the password is entered, only the menu items provided by the menu are available and the option to enter the GRUB shell or append or edit the entries is restricted. The following snippet of code illustrates how this is possible:

```
default=0
timeout=5
hiddenmenu
password=secret
```

If you do not like the idea of a clear text password in the GRUB menu file, then you can use the `grub-md5-crypt` command. You can add the encrypted password as follows:

```
default=0
timeout=5
hiddenmenu
password --md5 <password-hash>
```

You can also add a password directly to a stanza. Adding a password to a stanza ensures that users can only choose that selection from the menu if they know the password. In this way, should you want, you can always have a runlevel 1 entry in the menu but protected by the password as follows

```
title CentOS 6.5 Single User
  password --md5 <password-hash>
  root (hd0,0)
  kernel /boot/vmlinuz.version root=/dev/sda1 resume=/dev/sda2 1
initrd /boot/initramfs.version
```

Boot splashing with plymouth

As soon as we have begun the boot process and just prior to handing control to the kernel, a boot splash screen can be displayed. This, as the name suggests, controls the splash screen you may see during the boot process. In CentOS, this defaults to the plymouth theme: rings. Plymouth is the boot splash manager; we can use other themes should we wish. Some of these are installed as standard, while others are included in the standard repositories. Yet, more themes can be found in third-party repositories.

You can, of course, build your own theme. Essentially, a minimal theme is just a wallpaper.

Applying different themes

Most of the time during the boot process, you will not see the splash screen unless CentOS is your desktop machine. However, I would recommend still working with plymouth to change the default splash from rings to basic. With the basic theme, we can see the services loading during the boot process rather than the rings that merely show the boot progress. I would humbly suggest that if you are looking at the server during the boot process, then there are issues and you might want to see the services loading and messages they report back. If you want to be a little more relaxed in your approach, try the theme solar. This shows a planet and some asteroids whizzing around it to illustrate the boot process.

On the command line, we display the default theme as follows:

`$ plymouth-set-default-theme`

To display the available themes on the system, we can use the command as follows:

`$ plymouth-set-default-theme --list`

CentOS, by default, provides three themes as follows:

- **details**: This shows us the services as they load
- **rings**: This is the default theme and includes the CentOS logo with a spinning ring below the logo
- **text**: This is a blank splash screen with just the horizontal progress bar at the base of the display

These themes are all located in sub directories under the path: `/usr/share/plymouth/themes`. Should we want to change the theme to `details`, we can do so by using the following command. Please note that the command does take a few minutes to run as the process rebuilds the RAM disk to include the new theme.

```
# plymouth-set-default-theme --rebuild-initrd details
```

With this done, you can reboot and even see the difference as the system shuts down. Instead of the infernal rings, we see meaningful messages from our services as they close down.

If we want to be a little more adventurous, then standard CentOS repositories include the additional themes:

- fade-in
- solar
- spinfinity

In order to install and set the theme `spinfinity`, execute the following commands:

```
# yum -y install plymouth-theme-spinfinity
# plymouth-set-default-theme --rebuild-initrd spinfinity
```

A partial screenshot from the spinfinity theme is as shown in the following screenshot:

Summary

Well, here we are, we have made it to the end of another glorious chapter! You, my dear reader, yes you (there is only one of you), are a little closer to stardom in the Linux Hall of Fame.

We should now have been able to understand that GRUB is the bootloader commonly used in Enterprise Linux, and it will consist of stanzas to boot operating systems. Each stanza consists of three commands. The triumvirate of commands being root, kernel, and initrd. We also made sure we could edit the GRUB menu and solidly protect the GRUB console using passwords that are encrypted and unencrypted.

Finally, we ended up in the paddling pool, the watery shallows of Linux on a summer evening, learning to boot splash with plymouth. This decorated the dawn and dusk of a Linux day with a little color, or a lot of red in the case of spinfinity.

In the next section, we are going to walk into the Linux filesystems within CentOS, gaining an understanding of their makeup and structure. Starting with traditional systems based on disks or logical volumes, we will investigate how filenames relate to inodes and inodes relate to data. We will then move through to links, pipes, and sockets, and finally, finish off by taking a look at the **Better FS (btrfs)**.

3
CentOS Filesystems – A Deeper Look

So we know that our filesystems are comprised of files and directories; both of which are files, just different types. However, what about links, pipes, and sockets? What are they and how are they used? And why do we talk of links? What is the difference between a hard link and soft link? I think I need to sit down. I can feel one of my turns coming on.

Let's also challenge the traditional filesystem design; you may well have worked with a **logical volume manager (LVM)** in the past, but let me tell you just how last century that is. You are going to be blown away by the power and ease of your enterprise filesystem management using BTRFS, pronounced Better FS. We will cover the following sections in this chapter:

- **A magician's secret**: We reveal how to count subdirectories without actually counting them.

- **Special permissions**: This will cover the tail of the wall command and how it met the GUID bit.

- **Naming your pipes**: I am sure that you would not care to be unnamed, and your pipes feel this way too. We investigate how to use named pipes to enable **inter-process communication (IPC)**.

- **Understanding the command stat**: This will cover all you ever needed to know about an inode, the files' metadata.

- **Enterprise filesystem shootout**: In BTRFS versus LVM, BTRFS wins hands down. We look at what is new in the BTRFS and see how we can make use of snapshots and extend volumes.

A magician's secret

We know that there are many groups of people in this world that can and often do annoy us; magicians perhaps being just one of those groups of people. They annoy us because we do not know how they do what they do; quite simply we know that we are being tricked, but we don't quite know how. Well let me be the one to break the honor of the magician's circle and disclose a little trick within CentOS Linux that you can use to trick your colleagues; believe me when I say that this is one trick worth knowing.

Let me show you that if I run the following command on my CentOS 6.5 system, I will be shown a long listing of the specified doc directory:

```
$ ls -ld /usr/share/doc
```

The output on my system is as follows:

```
drwxr-xr-x. 758 root root 36864 May 1 09:09 /usr/share/doc
```

The first number that is displayed, 758, is the *link* count. This shows the number of filenames that are hard linked to the file's metadata; in simple terms, this directory has 758 separate names.

Immediately from this value, I can categorically state that this directory has 756 subdirectories!

> *"It's not rocket science, it is subtracting 2 from a number"*

The formula is simple! For a given directory, the number of subdirectories is equal to the hard link count of two.

I think it is time that we investigate this a little further. When a new directory is created, it is initiated with the link count being equal to two; in other words, each new directory has to have two names that point to it. This will consist of the directory name and the file named . (just the period by itself).

In fact, in a new directory, there are always two new files that are created along with the directory: the . and .. files.

- The . file represents the directory itself
- The .. file represents the parent directory

Try this yourself; it is easier to understand and might prevent you from going too dotty over this:

```
$ cd
$ mkdir newdir
$ ls -a newdir #Note the two files
$ ls -ld newdir # Note the hard link count of 2
```

The following screenshot shows the new directory and the listing of the two hidden files therein. The color coding, natural to BASH, highlights both files in blue, which indicate that they represent directories:

```
[andrew@centos ~]$ ls -a newdir/
```

I am sure, when you take time to think, that we use the dot notation as a form of shorthand all the time. Consider the following code using the copy command cp:

```
$ cp /etc/hosts .
```

Here, we copy the hosts file from the /etc directory to the current directory using the notation of a single dot. In the following example, we change to the parent directory using the cd command:

```
$ cd ..
```

We can now begin understanding how a directory's link count relates to the subdirectory count. If the filename consists of two dots representing the parent directory, then for each subdirectory we create in the given directory, we will have a new file pointing to the parent directory. Each of these double-dot files is hard linked to the subdirectory's parent directory.

Hard links

In Linux filesystems, we have two types of links: hard links and soft or symbolic links. Hard links are, as we have seen, the name or names of the file. A regular file will have just a single name when it is first created. We can add additional names to the file using the ln command:

```
$ cd
$ echo "Hello" > my_newfile
$ ln my_newfile the_samefile
$ ls -li my_newfile the_samefile
```

We will walk through the steps we executed on our system as follows:

1. We move to our home directory.

2. Then, we create a new file containing the word `Hello`.

3. The `ln` command links the original file to a new name, `the_samefile`. We now have two filenames that point to the same metadata. The hard link count of both files will be two; the names point to the same metadata.

4. Using the `ls` command with the option for the long listing, `-l`, will display the hard link count. The option, `-i`, will display the inode number of the file. The inode number of both files will be the same. As hard links share the same inode number, the source and target file must be on the same filesystem. An inode is an entry within a single filesystem.

Symbolic links

Symbolic links, or soft links as they are sometimes referred to, are completely separate files whose data points to another filename; as such, they can cross the filesystem boundaries and be a little more useful than hard links. Symbolic links have a file type of `l` indicating that they are a special type of file. Hard links are regular files and can only be identified as links via the hard link count. Symbolic links do not affect a file's hard link count; they are completely independent files with their own name, inode, and data. The data of a symbolic link is the pointer to the target files. In the following code segment, we can see the creation and display of a symbolic link:

```
$ cd
$ ln -s my_newfile the_linkedfile
$ ls -l the_linkedfile
```

Let's walk through the following steps that create a symbolic link in our home directory:

1. We first move to our home directory.

2. The `ln` command links the original file to a new name, `the_linkedfile`. The option `-s` will create a soft link.

3. Using the `ls` command, which is the option for the long listing, `-l`, we can see from the output that the first character, which indicates the file type, shows an `l` indicating that this file is a symbolic link. The extended output also shows where the target file is.

Special permissions

The permissions or *mode* of a file you we will be familiar with is **Read, Write, and eXecute (RWX)**. These permissions can be set to the three objects:

- User
- Group
- Others

The standard permissions are shown with their octal notation, should you want a quick revision exercise, as follows:

There is a fourth block of permissions that precedes user, group, and others. This block is for the special permissions; however, rather than representing RWX, the permissions comprise of:

- The set user ID (SUID) bit
- The set group ID (SGID) bit
- The sticky bit

Using symbolic notations, these permissions can be added to `file1`, which acts as our axiom for the filename during the following demonstration:

```
$ chmod u+s file1 #adding the SUID Bit
$ chmod g+s file1 #adding the SGID Bit
$ chmod o+t file1 #adding the Sticky Bit
```

The SUID bit

The set user ID bit is used when a program needs to run using another user ID other than the user running the program. When set, the program runs with the permissions of the file's owner and not the user ID of the current user. This is set on some simple programs; for example, the password program `/usr/bin/passwd` has this permission set. This is required as standard users can change their own password program but they do not have the permissions to write to the `/etc/shadow` file, where the passwords are stored. The program will always execute as the root user no matter who initiates it.

If you are curious and want to see how many files on your system have this permission included, then the `find` command may come to your aid:

```
$ find / -perm +4000
```

The command, as typed, will search the OS root directory, /, down for any file that includes the SUID bit, `-perm +4000`.

The SGID bit

Similar to the set UID bit, if the SGID permission is set on an executable, then the program will run with the group ID of the file's group rather than the group ID of the current user. This is set by default in the `/usr/bin/wall` file, and we will again take a closer look by executing the following command:

```
$ ls -l /usr/bin/wall
```

From the output, we see that the permissions read `r-xr-sr-x`. The lowercase s indicates that the SGID and execute permissions are set. If it were an uppercase S, then the execute permission would not be set for the group.

When looking at the `/usr/bin/wall` program, we should understand that this program is used to send messages to user consoles; it is a group owned by the `tty` group. With the SGID bit set, when any user executes this program, he or she run with the privileges of the `tty` group.

A user logged on to a console has some control over these messages using the y or n option with the `mesg` command:

```
$ mesg    #without options displays the current messaging state
$ mesg y #enables messages to be received in the console
$ mesg n #disables messages from being received in the console
```

We could leave the matter at this, understanding that we are simply enabling and disabling messages to our console. We could, but we would not learn the relationship with the SGID bit on the wall program, and we would not unlock the fountain of knowledge that understanding brings. Remaining within our console, we will determine which console we are currently connected to; the `tty` command will help us here. The output on my system shows /dev/pts/1. Obtaining a long listing of the device file using the following command will show the file type and permissions. The file type is c indicating a character device:

```
$ ls -l /dev/pts/1
```

From the output, we can see the permissions of the file; the group owner is `tty` and, if messaging is enabled, the group will have the write permission. If messaging is disabled, the group will have no permission. We can combine the two commands together using the bracket expansion we first saw in *Chapter 1, Taming vi*:

```
$ ls -l $(tty)
```

The contents of the brackets are evaluated first; the output from which is in turn processed using the `ls -l` command.

In the following screenshot, messaging is disabled as the group does not have the write permission to the console:

```
[andrew@centos ~]$ ls -l $(tty)
crw-------. 1 andrew tty 136, 1 May  4 15:35 /dev/pts/1
[andrew@centos ~]$ █
```

When we enable messaging and review the output in the following screenshot, we can see that, miraculously, the write permission now shows for the group:

```
[andrew@centos ~]$ mesg y; ls -l $(tty)
crw--w----. 1 andrew tty 136, 1 May  4 15:39 /dev/pts/1
[andrew@centos ~]$ █
```

We have now seen a little more of that initial Linux magic in which we indulged in earlier in this chapter. Moreover, we have seen how to apply it to real-world Linux issues by controlling the use of the /usr/bin/wall command via the /usr/bin/mesg command.

However, the giving from the SGID does not stop with executable files. The SGID bit can also be set on directories. When set on a directory, the SGID bit ensures that all new files created within the directory are group owned by the group owner from the directory. To put this in context, let's say that our web server's document root, (where the web pages go), is set to the `/var/www/html/` directory. If we set the group ownership of the directory to the `apache` group, we can then use the SGID bit to maintain the correct ownership of all files created. The following commands demonstrate this intricate procedure:

```
# chgrp apache /var/www/html
# chmod g+s /var/www/html
# ls -ld /var/www/html
```

Now, each new web page created in `/var/www/html` will automatically be group owned by the `apache` group. We have now seen that the SGID bit can be effective on executable files and directories.

The sticky bit

The final special permission is the sticky bit. This is used on directories and set on the `/tmp` directory during the default installation of CentOS. The ability to delete a file is controlled by directory permissions and not by, as some people think, the file's permissions. When you create or delete a file, you are writing to the directory. This means that within a central shared directory, such as `/tmp`, where all users can write to the directory, it would be possible for users to delete any file. To limit the deletions to files owned by the user, the sticky bit is applied to the directory. To add the sticky bit permission to the `/data` directory, we can use the following command:

```
# chmod +t /data
```

Naming your pipes

I am sure that we all have come across the vertical bar or pipe character `|`; we can use this to create command pipelines, where the output of one command is piped to the input of another. As a simple demonstration, we can use the following commands as an illustration of how often we may use unnamed pipes:

```
$ yum list installed | grep plymouth
```

The first command, `yum list installed`, lists all the installed packages which will be a considerable size; in order to reduce the content, we search for the string `plymouth` with the second command `grep`. The two lines of code are conjoined with an unnamed pipe. It is said to be unnamed as it is transient and only exists for the instance that the two commands run, which, incidentally, is much shorter than the life of a mayfly.

This transient nature may not be useful to us in every situation, in which case we can create named pipes, which are files with the pipe type. Files can be one of the following types:

- Regular file
- Directory
- Symbolic link
- Socket
- Named pipe
- Character device
- Block device

You should be quite familiar with the first three types, but we tend to see the others less, although we saw a character device file `/dev/pts/1` in the previous section where we were looking at the SGID bit. Character devices are simply terminals that we can access. Here, we want to keep our focus on the file type of pipe, some of which may exist in your filesystem already. We can hunt them using the `find` command, searching for a file type `p`:

```
$ find / -type p 2>/dev/null
```

Running this command as a standard user, you can expect errors related to directories to which we do not have rights; in such a case, it is often easier to redirect errors to `/dev/null`, as we have done here. Having the `autofs` service running on your system will create named pipes: `/var/run/autofs.fifo-misc` and `/var/run/autofs.fifo-net`.

Named pipes allow for different processes to talk with each other or interprocess communication. With unnamed pipes, the processes are always running in the same parent hierarchy, the same BASH shell in other words. As such, they are useful but only to us and our own parochial worlds. Named pipes, however, open up the input of one command to any process running on that system irrelevant of the process hierarchy. This is perhaps similar to the realization that you had when you first realized that there were more places in the world to holiday than the Isle of Wight. A service process such as the `autofs` service may connect to the output of the named pipe waiting for the input from clients on the system, releasing us from the inward facing coterie, which is the unnamed pipe, into a wider expanse of communication.

The easiest way to explain how named pipes operate is to demonstrate them. So why don't we open two terminal windows? These can be graphical terminals running on the desktop if this is easier. I will stay logged in through my own standard account into both windows.

In the first terminal window, we can type the following groups of commands:

```
$ cd  #move to your home directory
$ mkfifo my-pipe #create a named pipe called "my-pipe"
$ ls -l my-pipe #will list the file as type p
$ wc -l < my-pipe #We read in from the pipe and count the lines. As
nothing is connected to the input we wait for something to process.
```

While the first window waits for input, we can go to the second terminal window and feed data to the input of the pipe:

```
$ cd #move to your home directory where the pipe is located
$ ls > my-pipe #send the output of the ls command to the pipe
```

Immediately, we will see the result in the first window as we are now able to count the lines of output from the `ls` command that we input in the second terminal. By doing this, we have allowed two separate processes to talk with each other.

Understanding the command stat

The CentOS command line is full of tools, and trying to learn them all is perhaps a lifetime's work. As with all tasks, reaching the finish line begins with the first step. Our first step will be to delve into the world of the `/usr/bin/stat` command. By using this command, we can query a file's metadata. A file in CentOS consists of:

- A filename (hard link)
- File metadata (inode)
- Data

Using `stat` and the filename alone, we can view the complete inode metadata. This is demonstrated with the following group of commands:

```
$ cd #move to your home directory
$ ls > my_newfile #list the contents and redirect the output to the new file
$ stat my_newfile #display the inode metadata
```

The following screenshot displays the output of `stat`:

```
[andrew@centos ~]$ stat my_newfile
  File: `my_newfile'
  Size: 125          Blocks: 8        IO Block: 4096    regular file
Device: fd00h/64768d   Inode: 536029      Links: 1
Access: (0664/-rw-rw-r--)  Uid: (  500/  andrew)   Gid: (  500/  andrew)
Access: 2014-05-06 10:12:15.895980644 +0100
Modify: 2014-05-06 10:12:15.902981826 +0100
Change: 2014-05-06 10:12:15.902981826 +0100
[andrew@centos ~]$
```

We can see that the complete metadata is displayed, but if we choose, we can display just elements of the metadata; for example, to display the file permissions in the octal format, run the following command:

```
$ stat -c%a my_newfile
```

To display the permission in human-readable format, run the following command:

```
$ stat -c%A my_newfile
```

The output will show `664` and `-rw-rw-r`, respectively. The inode will always store the permissions in the octal format, but many commands, such as `ls` and `stat` can convert to a friendlier format.

There are three timestamps that are stored in the inode:

- The last access time
- The last modified time
- The last changed time

The last access time

The last access time for a file lists the time that the file was last read. This is dependent on the filesystem maintaining the last access time; there is a mount option noatime that prevents the last access time from being updated. To list the last access time for the file, run the following command:

```
$ stat -c%x my_newfile
```

The time shown for me is 10:12. If I now read the file and run the command again, the time will change:

```
$ less my_newfile
$ stat -c%x my_newfile
```

The time now shows as 10:28. This is useful to find out if files are being read on a system. If they are not, it indicates that perhaps they are not needed and can be archived onto another device.

The last modified time

The last modified time for a file indicates when the file itself was changed, that is, the file's data. If we edit the file and then check the last modified time, it will have changed.

```
$ ls >> my_newfile #we now append another listing to the file
$ stat -c%y my_newfile #displays the last modified time
```

This is now 10:36 as opposed to 10:12 when the original content was created.

 The output from ls -l also shows the file's last modified time.

The last changed time

The last changed time of a file relates to when the metadata was changed, as opposed to the file's data. Changing the file permissions, for example, will alter the last changed time:

```
$ chmod 640 my_newfile
$ stat -c%z my_newfile
```

The time for my system now shows that the file's metadata was changed at 10:41.

Enterprise filesystem shootout

The LVM has been for many years the way to manage disk growth, and allowing logical volumes to span over multiple disks and support backing up through the use of snapshots. LVMs, although very good, still require a filesystem to sit on top of the logical volume and hence, incur an extra level of management; bearing in mind that the LVM system itself has three levels of management:

- **Physical volumes**: These are the disk space made available to the LVM system
- **Volume groups**: These organize the physical volumes to be made available to the consumer
- **Logical volumes**: These consume the disk space made available via the volume groups and are presented to the filesystem tools to be formatted

Now just because we have used such software for the last 10 years or so does not give it the right to continue unchallenged, even within the enterprise. We now see **B-tree filesystem (BTRFS)** pronounced as **Better FS** making inroads in Linux. BTRFS is available on version 0.20 to install and can be used on CentOS 6.5, although caution should be taken, as it is marked as experimental.

What BTRFS has to offer

With over 55 kernel-based filesystems in the Linux kernel tree currently, do we really need another one? The first issue here is that many filesystems have limited or very specific usage; only the extN systems such as ext2, ext3, and ext4 are truly general purpose but even with the latest incarnation of these, ext4, the size limit is 16 TB. BTRFS scales to 16 **exabytes (EB)** and brings reliability features previously not found, as follows:

- Very fast filesystem creation
- Data and metadata checksums
- Snapshotting
- Online scrub to fix issues

Installing BTRFS

On the CentOS 6.5 demonstration system I am using, we will first need to install BTRFS:

```
# yum install -y btrfs-progs
```

Now that we have the utilities installed, we can begin to experience the power and simplicity of BTRFS. My lab machine currently has four additional free partitions on the second drive; each one consists of 1 GB to use in the following demonstrations.

Creating a BTRFS filesystem

To kick off the show today, we will first create a BTRFS filesystem on a single 1 GB partition, mount it to the /data directory, and copy some data to it as follows:

```
# mkfs.btrfs /dev/sdb5
# mount /dev/sdb5 /data
# find /usr/share/doc -name '*.pdf' -exec cp {} /data \;
# btrfs filesystem show /dev/sdb5
```

From these commands, you will see that we copy some of the existing PDF files to give us some real data to use in the demonstration, ensuring that we will see no loss of data during the exercises. The final command line shows the filesystem and confirms it size of 1 GB.

Expanding a BTRFS filesystem

We may well be running out of space within the /data structure; we are not but we can imagine. If we were using an LVM structure, we would have to run several commands to expand the existing filesystem across a new partition or disk. This would be the process in LVMs:

Volume management in the old way requires us to execute the following commands:

```
# pvcreate /dev/sdb6
# vgextend vg1 /dev/sdb6
# lvextend -L+1000M /dev/vg1/data_lv
# resize2fs /dev/vg1/data
```

Volume management with BTRFS

As we can see, there are four commands to be executed, all with a generous sprinkling of syntax that will try to trip us up. We can now see how to do this using BTRFS:

```
# btrfs add device /dev/sdb6 /data
```

That's it! That is all that we needed to do, and we now have a 2 GB volume. We can confirm this by using the following command:

```
# df -h /data
# btrfs filesystem show /dev/sdb5
```

Both commands will confirm that we now have 2 GB of disk space available in the volume and the data is still there and accessible. The volume metadata is copied to both partitions. In this way, we can view the volume information from either device:

```
# btrfs filesystem show /dev/sdb5
# btrfs filesystem show /dev/sdb6
```

Both commands will show the same data, as their metadata is stored on both devices.

Balancing the filesystem

If we had genuinely added the extra partition because we were running out of disk space within the original volume, then we can balance the data across the complete volume now as follows:

```
# btrfs balance start -d -m /data
```

The -m argument represents the metadata and -d represents the data. In this way, the disks are equally used.

Adding an entry to /etc/fstab

One would assume that we would like the /data directory mounted at boot time and we will add an entry to the /etc/fstab file. When mounting from this file, we must reference all the devices:

```
/dev/sdb5  /data  btrfs  device=/dev/sdb5,device=/dev/sdb6  0 0
```

In this way, we instruct the early mount process of the device construction when a BTRFS scan is not available.

Creating an RAID1 mirror

Software **redundant array of inexpensive disks (RAID)** is also support by BTRFS. The following are the currently supported RAID levels:

- RAID 0: Striping without redundancy
- RAID 1: Disk mirroring
- RAID 10: Striped mirror

We can create a mirrored device using BTRFS software mirroring, should we need it. This does not give us extra disk space, but does provide fault tolerance in the case of a disk failure. We can emulate this in our setup, but as all of our partitions are on one disk, it will not help against disk failure, but the idea holds true.

```
# mkfs.btrfs -m raid1 -d raid1 /dev/sdb7 /dev/sdb8
# mount /dev/sdb7 /mirror
```

Creating the mirror, we use RAID1 for the metadata and data -m and –d, respectively. The disk space available is 1 GB. Whatever we write to /dev/sdb7 is mirrored to /dev/sdb8; with mirroring, we lose 50 percent of the data storage but have a high level of redundancy.

We will again need to add an entry to the /etc/fstab file, as seen earlier to ensure the system mounts correctly during boot time:

```
/dev/sdb7   /mirror   btrfs   device=/dev/sdb7,device=/dev/sdb8   0  0
```

Using BTRFS snapshots

Analyzing what you have so far, BTRFS is quite cool, don't you think? However, we have not yet exhausted the wealth of goodness that it has to offer. Snapshots can be used as read only or read/write copies of data. The reality is that there is no need to copy data as it is effectively linked until it changes in one of the locations. In this way, a snapshot of a large filesystem can be taken instantly. You can use snapshots in the following ways:

- As part of a backup solution where you may be concerned with open files affecting the backup, the snapshot will be created as read only and subsequently you will implement a backup of the snapshot. In this way, the backup will be of the host filesystem at the point in time that the snapshot was created.

- Snapshots can be useful where you know many files will change in a structure and you may want to restore the original files quickly. Perhaps where you are working with scripts to modify many files, you can easily revert to the snapshot copies if the scripts prove not to be as robust as you had imagined, thought, or hoped.

The snapshot *must* be created in the same filesystem as the target data; as we mentioned before, the rapid creation of the snapshot is affected by a form of internal linking within the filesystem. Within a BTRFS filesystem, we can create subvolumes. Subvolumes allow discrete management identities within the BTRFS filesystem. We will take a snapshot of a BTRFS subvolume storing it in another subvolume on the same filesystem.

To achieve this, we shall define two subvolumes within the /data BTRFS filesystem. Defining the subvolumes will create both the directories in the filesystem as well as the BTRFS subvolume entities. We will create a snapshot of the first subvolume, storing it in the second subvolume on the same /data filesystem. We cannot create a snapshot of the complete filesystem as changes to the snapshot will need to be written back to itself casing infinite recursion; believe me infinite recursion is not a good thing, not a good thing, not a good thing,...

Let's begin by creating the two subvolumes:

```
# btrfs subvolume create /data/working
# btrfs subvolume create /data/backup
```

We can list subvolumes easily using the following command:

```
# btrfs subvolume list /data
```

With the subvolumes in place, we can now move our existing data to the /data/working directory, allowing some data to be ready for snapshotting. The working directory, as the name suggests, should be where our real data is stored and the lifeblood of our organization. If this data fails, then so does our organization and we lose our jobs. It makes sense that this data is managed carefully.

```
# mv /data/*.pdf   /data/working
```

Our scenario is that we test scripts that will delete files based perhaps on the last accessed time; I do realize that we should not be working with live data but living on the edge does liven up our otherwise mundane life. That said, we have not entirely lost all sense of the importance of this data. Before we run the scripts, we create a read-only snapshot of the data.

To create a read-only snapshot of the working subvolume, execute the following command:

```
# btrfs subvolume snapshot -r /data/working /data/backup/first-run
```

We can list the available subvolumes as shown earlier with the following command:

```
# btrfs subvolume list /data
```

From the output, we can see that the snapshot appears as a new subvolume. Listing the contents of both directories should indicate that the contents are the same:

```
# ls /data/working
# ls /data/backup/first-run
```

The name `first-run` is not important, but perhaps we can create multiple snapshots based on the data before the first run of the scripts, before the second run of the scripts, and so on. At this stage, the snapshot really does not take up any space as the data is the same in both the source and destination. Should we delete all the files from `/data/working`, the **copy-on-write** (**COW**) technology in BTRFS will then create the files in `/data/backup/first-run`. This would also be the case if the files were modified in any way rather than deleted; the snapshot holds the files as they were at the time the snapshot was created. We can simply copy the files back to the original location in the event of a catastrophe.

Summary

This chapter has seen us disseminate the filesystem structure that we find in CentOS Linux and opens our comfort zone to entertain new technologies such as BTRFS. We began with a little trickery or understanding of the hard link count that we can see with the `ls` or `stat` command. This count shows how many filenames are linked to the one inode or file metadata. Understanding the metadata of the file led us to look more at `/usr/bin/stat` and the options that it supplies to us including the three timestamps, not of the apocalypse but of the file itself: last access, last modified, and last changed.

A little foray into special permissions released the knowledge of how users can enable and disable console messaging, the console files being group owned by the `tty` group, and the write permission being added and removed.

Finally, we basked in the glory that is the BTRFS filesystem. This is truly something to start working with now as this will be the enterprise filesystem of choice for years to come. Providing both filesystem and volume management in a single task is simplified and improved beyond measure.

You now need to prepare yourself for the banquet that is YUM and of software repository management tool, Yellowdog Update Manager, ensuring that we know a little more than simply `yum install`.

4
YUM – Software Never Looked So Good

It is now time to encompass all that is good with the **Yellowdog Updater Modified (YUM)** software repository system, and the array of tools that we can use to make this work for us. YUM provides the power house behind the **Red Hat Package Manager (RPM)** software package. Without YUM, you, the administrator, will have to locate the RPM file to install and all of the dependency RPMs; YUM, on the other hand, will do this for you. You will learn valuable lesser known options, create your own RPM files, and add them to your own local repositories. In this chapter, we will go through the following sections:

- **Managing software installation with RPM files**: We will review the basics of the RPM package management.

- **Creating your own RPM file**: You will learn how to create an RPM file, learning more in the process of how software installation works with RPMs.

- **Using YUM**: We will discover the power of YUM and learn the skills needed to help us make the best use of our system and network.

- **YUM plugins**: We take an overview of YUM plugins and the extensions that can be added to this system.

- **Creating a YUM repository**: We will create our own repository using both standard software from CentOS and our own custom RPM. Having our own repository means that the installation source is a part of our system and we do not need to rely on external connections to install the software. We could also choose to share this with other hosts on our network to increase the benefits of our own repositories.

Managing software installation with RPM files

An element of Linux administration that can provide almost a daily dose of entertainment is managing the life cycle of software on your CentOS desktops and servers; this includes installing, updating, and removing software that can take the form of programs, documentation, and drivers, as well as more or less anything that consists of one or more files within Linux. Installing software using RPM files is preferable to install scripts. With an RPM-based installation, we can always query the database for information regarding what is currently installed on the system. Software removal is simplified because we have an inventory of what was added by the package and will require removal. The big downside of RPM management is the *dependency nightmare* we can find ourselves in when we try to install an RPM file that requires other software. We may well be able to locate the required RPM but for certain, there will be more dependencies to trace when we try to install the first dependency package.

A simple demonstration illustrating these issues would be to try and install the Foxit PDF reader; this is a lightweight alternative to the Adobe Reader. If we download the RPM file directly from the Foxit site http://www.foxitsoftware.com/downloads/, we can install, or try to install it on our CentOS desktop. The following command will almost certainly fail due to unmet dependencies:

```
# rpm -i FoxitReader-1.1-0.fc9.i386.rpm
```

We can list the dependencies using the following command:

```
 # rpm -qpR FoxitReader-1.1-0.fc9.i386.rpm
```

When I count the dependencies on my system, there are 32 dependencies to resolve directly from this RPM; other dependencies may show when we try to install these packages. This is going to take a long time to install using the rpm command alone. If we choose to use the following yum command to maintain the installation and are connected to repositories with the required dependency packages, we will find the whole process has just become a lot easier, and I can return to my golf!

```
# yum install FoxitReader-1.1-0.fc9.i386.rpm
```

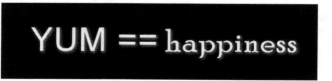

Reviewing some more of the basic RPM command-line syntaxes, we can list the following commonly used options:

- Install software from the RPM file: `rpm -i <example.rpm>`
- Uninstall RPM: `rpm -e <example>`
- Update the existing RPM or install if it is not installed. Additionally, display the progress as hash marks or percent: `rpm -Uvh <example.rpm>` or `rpm -Uv --percent <example.rpm>`
- List all the installed RPM-based software: `rpm -qa`
- List the RPM to which a file belongs: `rpm -qf /etc/hosts`
- List all files from an installed package: `rpm -ql <example>`
- List all files from an RPM file: `rpm -qpl <example.rpm>`
- To view the version of RPM: `rpm --version`

If you need to locate the RPM database, you will be able to find it in the `/var/lib/rpm` directory.

You may have noticed that when referencing an installed package, the RPM name can be used alone, whereas when using the `rpm` command with an RPM file, the complete filename and extension has to be used. The filename is made up from the following components:

`<package><version><release><architecture>.rpm`

For example, let's look at the RPM file for the **Z shell (ZSH)** package. The filename is:

`zsh-4.3.10-7.el6.x86_64.rpm`

- Package name: `zsh`
- Version: `4.30.10`
- Release: `7-el6`
- Architecture: `x86_64`

To verify this, query the package file using the `-i` or *information* option. In the following command, we use `-q` for query, `-p` for package, and the aforementioned `-i`.

`$ rpm -qpi zsh-4.3.10-7.el6.x86_64.rpm`

Creating your own RPM file

Even though I am advocating the use of YUM to manage software installations, we are still going to need RPM files. YUM is totally dependent on the underlying RPM files and infrastructure; the RPM file remains the software package that the yum command will install and these RPM files are instilled at the heart of the CentOS software management.

You might be able to cast your mind back to *Chapter 2, Cold Starts*, of this book when we were investigating Plymouth themes during the boot process; we are now going to create our own simple theme to brand our desktop or server with a corporate wallpaper during the system startup and shutdown. Once we have created the theme, the easiest way to install it across many systems is to distribute the theme as an RPM file. Later in this chapter, we will add the RPM to a YUM repository.

Creating the Plymouth theme

Firstly, we must create the theme, and with that completed, we shall be able to package it as an RPM file. Our theme will have three files contained within one directory. The directory needs to be added, along with the three files that it will house, into the themes folder of the target CentOS system, /usr/share/plymouth/themes.

The top-level directory that contains the three files for the theme is normally named after the theme to which it belongs. We are creating the tup directory to represent our theme as follows:

```
# mkdir /usr/share/plymouth/themes/tup
```

The theme, **The Urban Penguin (tup)**, will contain three files:

- 800.png: This is the wallpaper that will be shown as the splash screen. This has to be a PNG file.

- tup.plymouth: This is the master theme file that contains the theme manifest.

- tup.script: This is the action that the theme will run. This is the simplest form of a script-based theme, so we need this instruction file.

tup.plymouth

The tup.plymouth text file is the main theme file.

```
[Plymouth Theme]
Name=tup
Description=The Urban Penguin
ModuleName=script
```

```
[script]
ImageDir=/usr/share/plymouth/themes/tup
ScriptFile=/usr/share/plymouth/themes/tup/tup.script
```

As we can see in the preceding example, ModuleName being set to script means that we will need to ensure that we have the RPM plymouth-plugin-script listed as a dependency for our own RPM. We will build this into the RPM using the required directive during the build.

tup.script

The Plymouth script module will execute the tup.script file when the theme is running. The script that we create will just have one sprite. A sprite places elements on the boot splash, or the wallpaper that is seen during the system startup and shutdown. The wallpaper will scale to the size of the screen and take care to include the semicolons at the end of each line. The image used here is the 800.png file but you can use any PNG file that you add to the theme folder. Consider the following as a sample script:

```
wallpaper_image=Image("800.png");
screen_width=Window.GetWidth();
screen_height=Window.GetHeight();
resized_wallpaper_image=wallpaper_image.Scale(screen_width,screen_
height);
wallpaper_sprite=Sprite(resized_wallpaper_image);
wallpaper_sprite.SetZ(-100);
```

Creating the theme RPM

To build the RPM, we will work as a standard user, either through your own account or an account that is reserved specifically to build RPMs (if creating the account, just add the new account with standard privileges as a local or network account). Initially, we will need root privileges, though, to install the required packages for the build environment:

 # yum install -y rpm-build rpmdevtools

The previous command will install the tools that we will use to create the RPM. Using YUM, we will need to be able to connect to a repository that holds the software, but we do not need to be concerned with the location. With this in place, we can revert to the account that we will use to package the RPM. When logged in, we must make sure that we are in our home directory where we will create the top-level directories as follows:

$ cd

$ rpmdev-setuptree

This will create a `rpmbuild` directory with five subdirectories, which can be seen in the following screenshot:

```
[user@centos65 ~]$ tree rpmbuild/
rpmbuild/
├── BUILD
├── RPMS
├── SOURCES
├── SPECS
└── SRPMS
```

These directories become the working directories when building the RPM.

To begin, we will create the directory structure that we require below the SOURCES directory:

```
$ cd ~/rpmbuild/SOURCES
$ mkdir -p plymouth-theme-tup-1/usr/share/Plymouth/themes/tup
```

The top-level folder that we create is based on the name and version number that will represent the final RPM. The name will be `plymouth-theme-tup` and the version will be 1. The following directories represent the structure in the target filesystem; we need to target the /usr/share/plymouth/themes/tup directory.

With the directory in place, we can now copy the three files that constitute the theme into the newly created directory:

```
$ cp /usr/share/plymouth/themes/tup/* \
    plymouth-theme-tup-1/usr/share/plymouth/themes/tup
```

Now we need to create a gzipped archive of the folder structure; Within the ~/rpmbuild/SOURCES/ directory, we can run the following command to create the archive:

```
$ tar -czvf plymouth-theme-tup-1.tar.gz  plymouth-theme-tup-1/
```

The final stage before the build stage is to create the instruction or specs file. We can create this within the ~/rpmbuild/SPECS/ directory using our preferred text editor. We will call the ~/rpmbuild/SPECS/tuptheme.spec file:

```
Name: plymouth-theme-tup
Version: 1
Release: 0
Summary: TUP Corporate Theme
Group: System Environment/Base
License: GPL
```

```
URL: http://theurbanpenguin.com
Source0: plymouth-theme-tup-1.tar.gz
BuildArch: noarch
BuildRoot: %{_tmppath}/%{name}-buildroot
Requires: plymouth-plugin-script
%description
Corporate Plymouth theme displaying the TUP wallpaper

%prep
%setup -q

%install
mkdir -p "$RPM_BUILD_ROOT"
cp -R * "$RPM_BUILD_ROOT"

%clean
rm -rf "$RPM_BUILD_ROOT"

%post
echo ..
echo "Adding theme..."
%files
%defattr(-,root,root,-)
/usr/share/plymouth/themes/tup/800.png
/usr/share/plymouth/themes/tup/tup.script
/usr/share/plymouth/themes/tup/tup.plymouth
```

The file may seem complex, but most of the settings are self-explanatory. What's more? This can be used as a template for any RPM that is delivering text files, scripts, documentation, or pretty much any content that does not need to be compiled. If there were source files written in C that needed to be compiled, we would need to add a %build section.

For more information on the SPEC file, refer to the documentation that can be found at http://www.rpm.org/max-rpm/s1-rpm-build-creating-spec-file.html.

Now let's build us an RPM!

```
$ cd
$ rpmbuild -bb rpmbuild/SPECS/tuptheme.spec
```

The RPM file will be created in the `~/rpmbuild/RPMS/noarch/` directory. We can view this from the output of the command tree, as seen in the following screenshot:

```
[user@centos65 ~]$ tree rpmbuild/RPMS/
rpmbuild/RPMS/
└── noarch
        └── plymouth-theme-tup-1-0.noarch.rpm
```

We can verify that the files have been added correctly to the RPM. These are the three files that we need for the theme that we looked at earlier in the chapter and referenced within the `%files` section of the SPEC file:

$ rpm -qpl ~/rpmbuild/RPMS/noarch/plymouth-theme-tup-1-0.noarch.rpm

We should also verify the dependency that we added to the SPEC file using the `Requires` directive:

$ rpm -qpR ~/rpmbuild/RPMS/noarch/plymouth-theme-tup-1-0.noarch.rpm

The RPM cannot be installed now without the script plugin being present. If installed via YUM, then the dependency will automatically be resolved and installed as required.

Using YUM

As we have already seen with the Foxit PDF reader, the management of the RPM dependency requirements is greatly simplified by using YUM; almost certainly the ongoing software management of your CentOS will be based on YUM in the same way that **Advanced Packaging Tool (APT)** is used on Debian-based systems.

To install software with YUM, you do not need to know the filesystem path or even where the RPM file is. The required packages are located within software repositories, the location of which is configured within `/etc/yum.repos.d/` directory. Any file created in this directory should have the `.repo` extension.

On a standard build, these files will be directed to Internet-based software repositories; however, you can configure repositories locally on your own network, filesystem, or CD-ROM. This will be discussed later. For now, we will concentrate on the YUM commands:

- `yum install nmap`: Install the `nmap` package from a repository. We know this will be from a repository rather than a local file. For a local file, include the full filename and the `.rpm` extension and, if required, the path to the file. Earlier in this section, we saw how we could install the Foxit PDF reader RPM using YUM.

- `yum list nmap`: This will show the package and if it is installed or available. The output will also list the repository from which it was installed or is available from.

- `yum list installed`: This will list all the installed.

- `yum check-update`: This will show the available updates.

- `yum update nmap`: This will update just `nmap` if an update is available.

- `yum update`: This will update all the software on your system.

- `yum remove nmap`: This will uninstall the `nmap` package.

YUM plugins

Although YUM is one of the most used packaging systems, many users and administrators are not aware of the functionality that is available with the addition of plugins.

Using CentOS, and reading this book, you will now be very familiar with using the `yum` command to install packages and update your system. We have already seen how much we extend the RPM system with YUM, but that is no reason to ignore how much more is available.

Plugins are Python scripts or programs that extend the features that YUM offers. You will find the plugins located in `/usr/lib/yum-plugins`, and you will find that their configuration files reside under `/etc/yum/pluginconf.d/`. To be able to use any plugin, the plugins directive must be enabled in the YUM configuration file, `/etc/yum.conf`, as follows:

`plugins=1`

To search for the available plugins, we can use the following command:

`$ yum search yum-plugin`

On a standard build, CentOS will include the fastest mirror plugin, among others. This plugin performs very much as you may think, locating the fastest mirror repository in the time you download the packages. If enabled, this plugin is evoked automatically with the use of the `yum` command.

If you need to disable an individual plugin, rather than all plugins, then you will need to ensure that the enabled directive within the plugins' configuration file is set to `0`. For example, to disable the fastest mirror plugin, you will need to edit the `/etc/yum/pluginconf.d/fastestmirror.conf` file and configure the enabled line to read as follows:

`enabled=0`

The fastest mirror plugin is disabled. To enable the plugin, the settings should read as follows:

```
enabled=1
```

Another command plugin that is often installed is the `security` plugin. This is designed to be used in conjunction with the `yum` update commands:

- `yum --security check-update #List only security updates`
- `yum --security update #Install security updates only`

Creating a YUM Repository

The reasons to create a YUM repository are many. You can imagine a situation where you have more than one server on your network. It would make sense that the software is retrieved locally, rather than having all servers cross the WAN to access packages. The same reasoning scales to where CentOS desktops are common place. Centralizing software distribution is an absolute requirement, standardizing software being used and to ensure that your support team only has to support the single version of a package.

Building a local repository in a virtual machine that is just used for testing and development also makes great sense, removing the need to be connected to the network to install software packages. I ensure my classroom virtual machines always have a local file-based repository so that the system can be used as a discrete identity without relying on networking or external components.

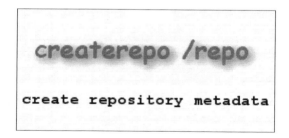

For this little foray, we shall create a local repository using the RPMs from the product DVD and we will use the command-line tool `/usr/bin/yumdownloader` in order to add additional required RPMs as follows:

1. Firstly, we will create a local directory to act as our local repository; to keep this simple, we just create a directory at the root of the filesystem and add RPMs directly into this folder:

   ```
   # mkdir /repo
   ```

2. With the product DVD mounted, we can populate the directory with the RPMs from the DVD:

```
# rsync -av /media/<volume name>/Packages/   /repo
```

3. We can add in the RPM what we created for the Plymouth theme earlier in this chapter:

```
# cp /home/user/rpmbuild/RPMS/noarch/plymouth-theme-tup-1-0.
noarch.rpm   /repo
```

4. With the network connectivity, we will download, not install, additional RPMS that are not on the DVD, which we require in our repository. The easiest way to achieve this is with the yumdownloader command:

```
# cd /repo;  yumdownloader --resolve kernel-source
```

5. The --resolve option will ensure that dependency packages are also downloaded. By default, they are downloaded to the current directory, so take care to move them into the /repo directory first:

6. We need to install the createrepo package:

```
# yum install createrepo
```

7. We are now ready to create the repository metadata that makes the file directory a repository:

```
# createrepo /repo
```

We have now been able to create a local repository; this will not be used until it is referenced by the YUM client. This will be achieved by the creation of a file with an extension of .repo within the /etc/yum.repos.d/ directory. For now, we can bask in the success of our creation. The real importance here is to take away the knowledge gained from using yumdownloader and the power that it brings to the repository creation being able to combine selected packages from multiple sources into the custom repository for you and your clients.

/etc/yum.repos.d/

Client systems need to be told about the location of their software sources or repositories and this is via the use of the .repo files. Although it is possible to define all of your repositories within the single file, /etc/yum.conf, it is more reasonable to add them as separate files in the directory as is detailed from the following excerpt from yum.conf:

```
# PUT YOUR REPOS HERE OR IN separate files named file.repo
# in /etc/yum.repos.d
```

The name of the file does not really matter, but the extension has to be `.repo`. We will create a file called `/etc/yum.repos.d/local.repo`:

```
[c6-local]
name=CentOS-6.5 - Local
baseurl=file:///repo
gpgcheck=0
enabled=1
```

The square brackets define the short name of the repository, and the name directive is really more of a description. The `baseurl` directive uses three forward slashes: two for the method of access, the file protocol in this case, and then the filesystem path slash itself. We have disabled public key checking (`gpgcheck=0`), but we could additionally sign the repository metadata should we wish to. The repository is enabled.

If this is the only repository that we would like to use, then we can move the existing repository files to a backup directory; this is probably easier than disabling the repositories by adding the `enabled=0` directive to each repository. Often, there is more than one repository defined per file, so the task is not simple. As I say, the easiest way is to move them to another directory and then add them back, should you later need access to the external repositories.

Having now defined the local repository within the `/etc/yum.repos.d/local.repo` file, we now effectively have access from YUM to all the RPMs that we have added to our own directory. Should we need to share this across a network to the other hosts on our internal network, it is a simple matter of adding a web server to provide access to the repository. Clients will then use `http://` `protocol` as the method of access.

Chapter 8, Nginx – Deploying a Performance-centric Web Server, will see us perusing the NGINX web server, and among other things we will learn how to direct a web server **Universal Resource Identifier (URI)** to this repository.

Summary

Congratulations! You have passed another milestone in reaching the end of this chapter and coming one step closer to the temple that is reserved for the most elite of administrators. We will now embark on a retrospective tour of this chapter in which we have gained some inside knowledge enabling us to manage software on our systems a little more effectively. Beginning with raw RPM files, we were able to see the strength in the management and inventory benefits that they provide, but the annoyance is in having to locate their dependencies. Liking the idea of RPMs, we ventured out to create our own RPM file to distribute and install a Plymouth theme; a theme that we have created to help brand our systems and reinforce our identity.

It was not long before that we then became more familiar with the YUM repository management system, which allows us to make the best use of the RPM inventory system but combining it with the ability to automatically resolve dependencies. This chapter culminated with the creation of our own local repository creating a standalone system being able to install software independent of any network connectivity.

In the next chapter, we will gain valuable skills to maintain service and process management on the CentOS 6.5 system. We will ensure understanding of the legacy System V services scripts as well as the new upstart system for service control. In addition, we will investigate tools that allow us to effectively manage processes running on the CentOS host.

5
Herding Cats – Taking Control of Processes

All too often, Linux administrators without the insight that you have, will leave services running as shipped after a Vanilla install of CentOS. We know how important it is to be able to justify each running process and service on systems that we manage, and in this chapter, you will gain the insight to manage this. While we are here, we will take a look at the new Upstart services that are replacing the System V scripts, which we have become so accustomed to. Here is a list of sections we will go through in this chapter:

- **Managing services with Upstart**: Investigate how to control services in CentOS 6.5 using Upstart and the /etc/init and /etc/event.d directories

- **Creating your own Upstart script**: Learn how to create custom startup script for Upstart to manage your own needs at system boot

- **Managing processes**: Gain practice with the p series of tools from the package procps to manage running processes: ps, pstree, pgrep, pmap, and pkill

Managing services with Upstart

For many years now, we have become used to managing services with System V init scripts that date back many years. However, without the desire to improve and the dedicated meliorism of so many in the open source community, we would not move on and improve. In CentOS 6.5, we now see some services being managed from the configurations within the /etc/init directory. These services make use of Upstart. This may be short-lived, as the beta release of Red Hat Enterprise Linux 7 uses a similar service manager, systemd, which is likely to prevail over Upstart. That said, both Upstart and systemd are managed in a very similar way, so visiting Upstart here is not an issue.

Firstly, we can check to see that we are indeed using `upstart` using the following command:

```
# yum list upstart
```

The output from the preceding command should list the package as being installed. The service uses the `/etc./init` directory for its configuration and from here, we can see the services that utilize Upstart. Using the `rpm` command, we can check which package created this directory:

```
# rpm -qf /etc/init
```

The output shows the directory belonging to the `upstart` package. On CentOS, we have just a few services that are controlled via Upstart; however, we will see that it is very easy to configure our own services as required using this mechanism.

Within the `/etc/init` directory, we can see that the consoles screens are managed by `upstart` with the `tty.conf` file, and we can also see the `splash-manager.conf` file. This service is enabled for reboot and poweroff, runlevel 0 and 6, to request the Plymouth splash screens (remember Plymouth from *Chapter 2, Cold Starts*). The beauty of both Upstart and systemd is that we do not need to manage the symbolic links in the run control directories the way we required with older System V scripts. Taking a look inside the `/etc/init/spash-manager.conf` file, we can see when the service will run and that this is provided directly without reference to the old symbolic links. The following is an example of an Upstart directive:

```
start on starting rc RUNLEVEL=[06]
```

The preceding line states that Upstart will run the scripts contained in the configuration file on starting and on changing to runlevel 0 and 6. It is as simple as that. The configuration may also contain everything that is required to run the service; this file becomes the autonomous service we have been looking for, self-contained in the single configuration file.

Creating your own Upstart script

One of the best ways in which you can learn about these services is to create your own configuration file containing the Upstart script and all the associated conditions for our service. The configuration file will require the extension of `.conf` and has to be created in the `/etc/init` directory. For the purpose of this demonstration, we will create a simple service with the well-researched and inventive name: `sample`.

Using the text editor vi to create the `/etc/init/sample.conf` file, the service begins
to take shape:

```
#/etc/init/sample.conf
description "Simple demonstration upstart script"
author "The Urban Penguin"
start on runlevel [35]
script
  logger -p local1.info "Starting upstart service"
end script
```

The service itself does nothing other than use the logger program to write to the
syslog daemon; we can read the output from the `/var/log/messages` logfile. You,
of course, could adjust the service to do more; however, this acts as a great start in
demonstrating how compact the services can be.

We can test the service using the `/sbin/initctl` command:

```
# initctl start sample
```

```
# tail -n 1 /var/log/messages
```

The service can be manually started as we have shown here, if not manually started,
it will start automatically, or at least send the message to the logfile when the system
enters runlevel 3 or 5.

```
#/etc/init/sample.conf
description "Simple Upstart script"
author "The Urban Penguin"
start on runlevel [35]
script
        logger -p local1.info "Starting upstart service"
end script
~
```

Along with the script option that we used here, we can additionally run pre or post
scripts, especially useful where the service is a binary and we need to endure a
certain environment in which it can run. There is an `exec` directive that can be used
in place of the `script` directive where a single binary should run in place of the
script. The full life cycle of an upstart service includes:

- Pre-start
- Post-start
- Main (using exec or script)
- Pre-stop
- Post-stop

The advantages that we gain from using Upstart and/or systemd is that we are no longer restricted to only starting services for given runlevels; we can also start these services for events such as disks (or block devices) being added or other services being started. Many of these event driven services can be found in the /etc/event.d directory.

We can control Upstart services using the /sbin/initctl command. To view the options available, the following command can be used with the help option:

```
# initctl help
```

The output will show that the version option can be used to check the version of Upstart in use, as seen in the following screenshot:

```
[root@centos65 event.d]# initctl version
init (upstart 0.6.5)
[root@centos65 event.d]# 
```

Managing processes

The bulk of this chapter will visit the procps package and the p series commands that we can use to manage our processes to make sure that we can fully appreciate the power that these tools can offer from the command line.

Many administrators are accustomed to using the ps command to determine the running process, and often the output is then piped to grep to search for a given process name. Although there is nothing incorrect with this as such, we may prefer to use tools that streamline these steps and are specifically designed tools for the purpose. For the moment, we will ignore the /ps command in preference of more specific tools with a real purpose to their binary lives.

Using the pgrep command

The /usr/bin/pgrep command really does become a snap-in replacement for the ps and grep pipelines we use all too often. For example, if I start my Apache web server, I can easily check the **Process IDs (PIDs)** in use by the service:

```
# service httpd start
# pgrep httpd
```

The output of the command follows:

```
[root@centos65 event.d]# pgrep httpd
3950
3953
3954
3955
```

From the output, I can see the lowest PID, in my case **3950**. This will be the main daemon process that will spawn the child processes. Knowing how much we enjoy the easy life, we can see how effortlessly we can the child processes to the parent using the pstree command with the parent process as the argument. There are eight child processes in my case, no need to use my thumbs to count these.

 # pstree 3950

Here's the output to the preceding command:

```
[root@centos65 event.d]# pstree 3950
httpd──8*[httpd]
[root@centos65 event.d]# █
```

Using the pstree command

This utility is so under used; I am sure that many administrators just know to execute the command without arguments or options. We have seen with the previous example how powerful it can be, but of course there is much more.

The pstree command, when run without arguments or options, will list the process tree from PID 1 through all running processes showing each in a hierarchical form linked by **parent process ID (PPID)** and PID.

To take it a step further, we can use the -h option, which will highlight the process tree in which we run pstree:

$ pstree -h

The following screenshot shows the highlighted extract from `pstree`:

```
├─gnome-screensav
├─gnome-settings-──{gnome-settings}
├─gnome-terminal──┬─bash──su──bash──┬─pstree
                  ├─gnome-pty-helpe
                  └─{gnome-terminal}
```

We can see from the previous screenshot that we have run `pstree` from a `gnome-terminal` in which we had been running the Bash shell in a **substituted user (SU)** environment; it is all laid out clearly for us to see.

Running something similar, we can highlight the process tree for the `httpd` process running at PID 3950 using the following command:

```
$ pstree -h 3950
```

On my system, this can be seen in the following extract from the screenshot:

```
├─httpd──8*[httpd]
├─im-settings-dae
├─login──bash
```

Using `pstree` with the `-a` option will show the process and any arguments used when it was started. This can be useful to see that a service is taking the correct configuration options:

```
$ pstree -a
```

Using the pkill command

When we reconsider from where we started this chapter, with the understanding that many administrators are accustomed to using the `ps` command and piped to `grep`, we should question the need to run the `ps` command in the first place. Perhaps we do this in order to kill a process. We did show earlier in this chapter how we can simplify and streamline the `ps`/`grep` pipeline with `pgrep`; the reality though, is that, we can streamline it further with `pkill`. Let's assume that we are running CentOS as a desktop, and while running the Firefox web browser we notice that is has become unresponsive, we can simply use the `pkill` to resolve the issue:

```
$ pkill firefox
```

Of course, the process names in Linux are case sensitive, but you do get used to the names of those processes that you may often need to whip into shape with a little `pkill`.

We can also kill all processes owned by a particular user. They may have done something really bad, and their session is totally unresponsive. We could try:

```
# pkill -9 -U bob
```

The preceding command will send the kill signal (-9) to all processes owned by the user bob.

If it is just processes in one terminal that we need to concern ourselves with, then we could use the following command:

```
# pkill -9 -t tty2
```

This will kill all processes running in the `tty2` console. If we own the running processes, we can execute the `pkill` command as our own account. If we don't own those processes, then the commands need to be run as root. We have been using the -9 signal in the last few examples, as we want to be sure to remove all process. It may be better to run the commands in the following way for best practice:

```
# pkill -15 -t tty2
# pkill -9 -t tty2
```

In this way, we issue the terminate signal first (-15) and then the kill (-9). In this way, processes are shutdown gracefully if they respond to the initial terminate request; those that are unresponsive to the terminate signal are then cleaned up with the final kill.

Just because a process does not respond to the terminate request, it does not mean that the process has hung; the bash shell, for example, does not respond to a terminate request, it has to be killed outright. This is just how the program is written.

To see a list of signals that can be issued, we should use the `/usr/bin/kill` command with the -l (list) option as follows:

```
$ kill -l
```

An extract from the output can be seen in the following screen capture:

```
[user@centos65 Desktop]$ kill -l
 1) SIGHUP      2) SIGINT      3) SIGQUIT     4) SIGILL      5) SIGTRAP
 6) SIGABRT     7) SIGBUS      8) SIGFPE      9) SIGKILL    10) SIGUSR1
11) SIGSEGV    12) SIGUSR2    13) SIGPIPE    14) SIGALRM    15) SIGTERM
16) SIGSTKFLT  17) SIGCHLD    18) SIGCONT    19) SIGSTOP    20) SIGTSTP
21) SIGTTIN    22) SIGTTOU    23) SIGURG     24) SIGXCPU    25) SIGXFSZ
```

Although many possible signals exist, they must be written into the program if it is to respond to the signal. This is where the -9 or -sigkill option is useful, although abrupt, the signal works directly with init to remove the process rather than relying on the application to respond.

Using the pmap command

Another useful tool from the procps package that we can use to gain information on running processes is the pmap command. This can be used to print a memory map for a running process. In simple terms, it will show you how much memory is being used by the process and any library modules that it uses.

To gain information on the PID for the current shell, we can use the special variable $$; thus, pmap $$ will show me the process map for my current shell:

```
$ pmap $$
```

The output looks most impressive; firstly we see that $$ on this system resolves to the PID 7259 and /bin/bash. As the process map continues, we see the address column followed by the size of memory in use by each component of /bin/bash.

From the following partial screenshot, we can see the output that you can expect from the pmap command:

```
[user@centos65 Desktop]$ pmap $$
7259:   /bin/bash
0000000000400000      848K r-x--  /bin/bash
00000000006d3000       40K rw---  /bin/bash
00000000006dd000       20K rw---    [ anon ]
00000000008dc000       36K rw---  /bin/bash
```

Summary

In this chapter, we have been able to while away a little boondoggle time, learning about the `procps` package in CentOS Linux and all the treasures that it can reveal. The tools therein are a gold mine to administrators and can save us all valuable time where we elect the most effective tool to be used in the examining processes. Putting this into practice, we have seen the effortless use that can be made from the `pgrep` and `pkill` commands in streamlining our process management, while tools such as `pmap` are more useful for diagnosing system resource usage.

As we get ready to venture into the next chapter, we will look at some of the valuable shortcuts that we can use when managing users on a CentOS 6.5 system.

6
Users – Do We Really Want Them?

The question, I admit, is more than a little rhetorical but there are times when we dream of how great our lives would be without pesky users getting in the way and gumming up the cogs that make our systems run; however, the better we manage the user base on our Linux systems, the better CentOS will be to us. In reality, the more control we have over the users, the more life is better for them as they can continue their work uninterrupted by system downtime.

In this chapter, we will develop techniques to maintain unobtrusive control of our systems, keeping ourselves sane and the users happy. This will include:

- **Managing public and private groups**: Understanding how we can use public groups and overriding the CentOS default of private groups can give us more scope in assigning permissions to users. We have to be aware of the potential pitfalls to each solution.

- **Getent**: This can provide us with a global view of our users and groups and will open up to us in this chapter the understanding of the name services switch file: `nsswitch.conf`.

- **Quotas**: Using quotas can allow us to both monitor and if required, restrict users' space to a partition, and is truly important where users' home directories are located.

- **Scripting user creation**: When creating a user, we will need to set the password and possibly user's disk quota limits; it makes sense then to combine all these activities into a script so that nothing is forgotten.

Managing public and private groups

The Red Hat and, therefore, the CentOS user management systems deploy a private user group system. Each user created will also belong to an eponymous primary group; in other words, creating a user bob will also create a group bob, to which the user will be the only member.

Linux groups

Firstly, we have to understand a little about Linux groups. A user has both a primary group and secondary groups.

User ID and group ID (UID/GID) are used with the permission management structure in Linux. Every file in any filesystem will be owned by a user and a group by means of storing the UID and GID in the files metadata. Permissions can be assigned to the user, group, or others.

Each user has one UID and GID but belongs to just one group, which is a little restrictive, so users additionally have secondary groups. Users can change their current GID to one from their secondary groups using the /usr/bin/newgrp command, effectively switching their GID. In practice, this is not required and leads us to describing the differences between the users' primary group and secondary groups.

When creating a new file, the users UID and their current GID are used to create the ownership of the new file. If a user creates a new file, he/she will be the owner of that file and the file will be group owned by his/her own private group, creating an inherently secure system without the need of user intervention. Secondary groups are used in all other situations when accessing resources that *currently* exist. Users present all of their secondary groups when accessing a resource. In this way, a file that is readable by the users group but not to others will be accessible to a user whose GID is set to his/her own private group, but the list of secondary groups to which they belong includes the users group.

When assessing a user's ID, setting the /usr/bin/id command can be very useful. Run without any options or arguments and the output will display your own associated IDs. In the following screenshot, we can see that the user andrew belongs to only the private user group and has no additional secondary group memberships:

```
$ id
```

```
[andrew@centos65 ~]$ id
uid=504(andrew) gid=504(andrew) groups=504(andrew)
```

We will use the same command but this time we will use the user, u1, as an argument. The output will show the associated IDs of that account; this command can be run as a standard user:

```
$ id u1
```

From the following screenshot, we can see that the user, u1, has the primary group or GID assigned to the private group u1; however, u1 additionally belongs to the users group.

```
[user@centos65 etc]$ id u1
uid=501(u1) gid=501(u1) groups=501(u1),100(users)
[user@centos65 etc]$ ▮
```

With the current IDs in place for the user u1, any new file created will be group owned by GID 501 (u1), but u1 can access any resource accessible to the users and u1 groups without any additional action on u1's part. From an administrative perspective, we need to make sure we assign the correct secondary IDs to our users.

The same cannot be said for the first example that we looked at. The user, andrew, currently belongs only to andrew's private group, so he can only access resources where permissions are set to:

- Their UID (andrew)
- Their private GID (andrew)
- Others

The user account andrew does not have access to permissions assigned to the users group in the same way that the user u1 does.

Adding users to groups

We can now see that the user u1 has the desired access to resources shared with the users groups, but what about andrew? How can we help here?

If the user already exists and we need to add him/her to a public group, then we can use the usermod command to add the user to an additional group. When we add andrew to the users group, we will also want to maintain any existing secondary groups' memberships.

Run the following command:

```
# usermod -G users andrew
```

If we choose to run the preceding command, then `andrew` would be added to the `users` groups but, along with his primary group, this would be his only secondary group membership. In other words, if `andrew` belongs to multiple secondary groups, the `-G` option overwrites this group list, which is not a good thing.

The command ID can display current secondary groups with the `-G` option:

```
# id -G andrew
```

If we combine the two commands together, then we can effectively append the `users` groups to the current group list of `andrew`. To do this, additionally, we have to translate the spaces in the group list supplied by the command ID into commas:

```
# usermod -G$(id -G andrew | tr ' ' ','),users
```

The commands in the parenthesis are evaluated first. The `id` command creates a space-separated list of secondary groups, and the `tr` command will translate the spaces to commas (in this case). The group list we supply to `usermod` needs to be comma delimited but can use group names or IDs. More simply though, we can use the append option to usermod as shown in the following code example:

```
# usermod -a -G users andrew
```

When creating new users, we can simply specify the secondary groups the user should belong to. We don't need to concern ourselves with the existing group membership:

```
# useradd -G users u4
# id u4
```

From the following output, we can see that the new user, `u4`, is created and added to the secondary group users.

```
[root@centos65 ~]# useradd -G users u4
[root@centos65 ~]# id u4
uid=505(u4) gid=505(u4) groups=505(u4),100(users)
[root@centos65 ~]# 
```

Evaluating private group usage

You do not need to use private `groups` schemes. They are the default, but as with all defaults, we can specify options to modify this. Using the `-N` option with `useradd` will not create the private groups and, if not specified, the user's primary group or GID will be the `users` groups. Let's execute the following commands:

```
# useradd -N u5
# id u5
```

The output is shown in the following screenshot, and we see that the users' primary group is the `users` group:

```
[root@centos65 ~]# useradd -N u5
[root@centos65 ~]# id u5
uid=506(u5) gid=100(users) groups=100(users)
[root@centos65 ~]#
```

The only security issue that we may need to contend with is that now, by default, any file created by the user u5 will be group owned by a shared group. Depending on the circumstances, this may be not desirable; however, having all files private to the user by default is no more desirable either. This is up to the administration team deciding which model suits the organizational needs best.

Getent

The `/usr/bin/getent` command will display a list of entries, *Get Entries*. The entries are resolved by *Name Service Switch Libraries*, which are configured in the `/etc/nsswitch.conf` file. This file has a list of databases and libraries that will be used to access those databases.

For example, we could use the `getent passwd` command to display all users, or `getent group` to display all groups. We could extend this though to commands such as `getent hosts` to display host file entries and `getent aliases` to display user aliases on the system.

The `nsswitch.conf` file will define the libraries used to access the `passwd` database. On a standard CentOS system, `/etc/passwd` is often the only local file, but an enterprise system could include **Lightweight Directory Access Protocol (LDAP)** modules. In the next chapter, we will learn more using directory services.

We search the `/etc/nsswitch` file for the `passwd` database using `grep`:

 # grep passwd /etc/nsswitch.conf

We can see that on my system, we just use the local files to resolve user names:

```
[root@centos65 ~]# grep passwd /etc/nsswitch.conf
#passwd:    db files nisplus nis
passwd:     files
[root@centos65 ~]#
```

The getent command is a very useful way to quickly list users or groups on your system, and the output can be filtered or sorted as required with the grep and sort commands. For example, if we want to see all configured groups on our system that start with the letter u and have only one additional character in their names, we can use the following command:

```
# getent group | grep 'u.:' | sort
```

The following screenshot shows this command:

```
[root@centos65 ~]# getent group | grep '^u.:' | sort
u1:x:501:u1
u2:x:502:u1,u2
u3:x:503:
u4:x:505:
```

Quotas

In almost all areas of user management, we have to assign disk space quotas of some description in order to give the responsibility of disk space management back to the user. If we do not, then the user would never know the struggles that we have to face in providing them with unlimited disk space. Allowing the user to see that their space is filling up then may prompt them to carry out a little housekeeping.

In Linux, disk quotas are applied to the mount points; if you want to limit a user's space in their home directory, then the /home directory will need to be in its own partition. If it is part of the root filesystem, then a user's space will be restricted to all directories within that partition.

Quota restrictions are implemented using tools from the quota package. You can use the yum command to verify that it is installed:

```
$ yum list quota
```

If the output of the command indicates that it is available rather than installed, then install the quota with:

```
# yum install quota
```

Setting quotas

My system includes a partition for /home and has the quota package installed. We now need to set the correct mount options for the /home partition. Currently, it does not include quotas.

To enable this, we will edit the /etc/fstab file and mount options for the /home partition. The following two mount options should be added to enable journal quotas for a selected partition:

`usrjquota=aquota.user,jqfmt=vfsv0`

The usrjquota=aquota.user part specifies the quota file, and jqfmt=vfsv0 specifies the quota format.

The line in question is shown in the following screenshot:

```
17 /dev/sdc1  /home  ext4 defaults,usrjquota=aquota.user,jqfmt=vfsv0 0 2
```

We have enabled journal-based user quotas as we are using ext4, a journal-based filesystem. User space restriction is checked when writing the journal rather than waiting until the changes are flushed to disk. We also set the format of the journal quotas.

To make these settings effective, we can remount the /home partition using the following command:

`# mount -o remount /home`

We will now need to initialize the quota database; this was referenced in the mount options as aquota.user and will reside at the root of the partition where quotas are enabled. Enabling quotas on a filesystem may take some time, depending on the amount of data in the filesystem:

`#quotacheck -muv /home`

Using these options with the /sbin/quotacheck command, we can set the following options:

- -m: This indicates not to remount as read-only during an operation
- -u: This is for user quotas
- -v: This is the verbose output
- /home: This is the partition to work with, or use -a for all quota-enabled partitions

It may be worth adding the `quotacheck` commands and options into your `crontab` to ensure that `quotacheck` is run perhaps once a day. Even though journal quotas are more reliable than traditional quotas, there is no harm in re-evaluating file space used to ensure that the data maintained is accurate.

Quotas can be set with the `edquota` or `setquota` command; I prefer the `setquota` command, but traditionally `edquota` is taught to new administrators. The `/usr/sbin/edquota` command takes you into your editor to make the changes, whereas `/usr/sbin/setquota` sets the quota directly from the command line:

```
# setquota -u u1 20000 25000 0 0 /home
```

The preceding command will set the quota for the user `u1`. Giving the user a soft limit, just a warning when they exceed 20 M (20 x 1k blocks) and implementing a hard limit of 25 M, where the user cannot save any more data in `/home`. I have not limited the user `u1` with either soft or hard limits to the number of files they may have, just the space they use.

The `/usr/sbin/repquota` command can be used to display disk usage:

```
# repquota -uv /home
```

The output from my system is shown in the following screenshot:

```
[root@centos65 ~]# repquota -uv /home
*** Report for user quotas on device /dev/sdc1
Block grace time: 7days; Inode grace time: 7days
                        Block limits                File limits
User            used    soft    hard  grace    used  soft  hard  grace
----------------------------------------------------------------------
root        --      20       0       0            2     0     0
user        --   31072       0       0          349     0     0
u1          --      36   20000   25000            9     0     0
u2          --      32       0       0            8     0     0
u3          --      32       0       0            8     0     0
andrew      --      36       0       0            9     0     0
u4          --      32       0       0            8     0     0
u5          --      32       0       0            8     0     0

Statistics:
Total blocks: 7
Data blocks: 1
Entries: 8
Used average: 8.000000
```

Scripting user creation

User creation will now consist of three steps:

- useradd: This creates the user
- passwd: This sets the password
- setquota: This sets the disk limits

We can ensure that all this happens correctly and uniformly using scripts to ensure the procedural integrity of the user creation process. It is also going to save you time. As a very quick solution, the following script provides all that we need:

```
#!/bin/bash
useradd -m -G users $1
echo Password123 | passwd --stdin $1
passwd -e $1
setquota -u $1 20000 25000 0 0 /home
```

We will need to run the script with the new username as the argument, as shown in the following example:

```
# userscript.sh bob
```

Reading the script though line by line can explain the script contents as follows:

- #!/bin/bash: This is the script interpreter to use
- useradd -m -G users $1: This creates the user supplied as the first argument to the script, $1. The user's home directory will be created, and it will be added to the users group.
- echo Password123 | passwd --stdin $1: This sets the user's password to a standard password.
- passwd -e $1: The password is expired so the user will need to set their own password when they first login.
- setquota -u $1 20000 25000 0 0 /home: Finally, the quotas are implemented for the user.

We can, of course, allow more functionality in the script to set different groups and quotas; however, as an example of procedural integrity and a functional script, this is a great start.

Summary

As we close another chapter, we can take stock of all that we have acquainted ourselves with in the process. The big task for this section was to become more accustomed to the vagaries of CentOS group management and being able to properly differentiate between the primary group and secondary groups of a user. During this process, we took the time to evaluate the use of public and private group schemes and the use of the -N option to disable the user's private group during user creation.

It was not long before we found ourselves in the depths of /etc/nsswitch.conf and the getent command (get entries). From here, we got down straight to business implementing user disk limits or quotas before seeing how to link all of this together with scripts.

In the next chapter, we stick to the theme of users, but look at centralizing our accounts in a central LDAP directory, using the open source code from Red Hat's directory server by implementing the 389 Directory Server on CentOS 6.5.

7
LDAP – A Better Type of User

Having a local user account and password defined on each server and workstation for your access is not really practical. Imagine trying to enforce password changes when you may have to implement the change on 10 or 12 systems that you may use. You may also wish to consider what happens when a user leaves; do you really think the account will be deleted from every system each time? The reality is that where multiple systems are placed, some form of directory solution must be in place; this may be means of OpenLDAP, or even Active Directory. Yes, CentOS can join a Windows domain. We will look at 389-ds, the CentOS implementation of the Red Hat Directory Server. 389-ds is based on OpenLDAP, but with some pretty smart management tools. We are going to cover the following topics in this chapter:

- **LDAP concepts**: In this section, you will understand terms that are used when talking about directory services
- **Installing 389-ds**: This section involves installing the 389 Directory Server ensuring all the plumbing is in place
- **LDAP user account management**: This section includes the management life cycle of users in the directory
- **LDAP authentication**: This section will cover authenticating a second CentOS server to the shared directory

LDAP concepts

LDAP stands for Lightweight Directory Access Protocol; as the name suggests, it began as a client-server protocol used to access a directory, but there was so little development in directories that it soon took on the entire role of a directory server. If we break a directory down, the **Directory Access Protocol (DAP)** is just one small part of the many pieces of an LDAP server:

- **Directory Information Database (DIB)**: This is the database where the directory is stored

- **Directory Information Tree (DIT)**: This is the hierarchical organization that represents entries in the DIB, organizations, organizational units, and so on
- **Directory System Protocol (DSP)**: This represents the server to server communication
- **Directory Access Protocol (DAP)**: This represents the client-to-server communication
- **Directory Server Agent (DSA)**: This is the server software
- **Directory User Agent (DUA)**: This is the client software
- **Directory Information Shadowing Protocol (DISP)**: This is the replication of the directory
- **Schema**: These are entry data definitions

Each of these elements is represented in some way in all LDAP directories and common directories, including OpenLDAP, Red Hat Directory Server, and 389-ds. We will be looking at the 389-ds, which is based on the Red Hat Directory Server, which in turn is an implementation of OpenLDAP with some enhanced features. Ultimately, directories are used in the creation of what has commonly been dubbed as identity management, the central storage of user accounts to lessen the burden on account management, and improve security. A user is much more likely to recall a strong password if he/she only remembers a single credential set.

Installing 389-ds

In the following sections, we will see the steps involved in installing 389-ds.

Configuring DNS or hostname records

When installing OpenLDAP or 389-DS, it is imperative that you can resolve the hostname of the system on which you install the directory. My system is named `ldap1.tup.com`, and I have a local DNS record for this but it can also be maintained by an entry in the local `/etc/hosts` file on the host system. I can verify the name is correct by using the `host` command or something similar:

```
$ host ldap1.tup.com
```

You should see the IP address being returned. You can see the result of this command when executed on my system in the following screenshot:

```
[andrew@ldap1 Desktop]$ host ldap1.tup.com
ldap1.tup.com has address 192.168.0.76
[andrew@ldap1 Desktop]$ ▌
```

Setting TCP keepalives

The default timeout of TCP connections is 120 minutes. We will configure it for five minutes. In doing so, we will reduce the overhead caused by dropped TCP connections; they will be closed much more quickly. Edit the /etc/sysctl file to include the following line:

```
net.ipv4.tcp_keepalive_time = 300
```

Load the settings using sysctl to make them current as well as the default for the next reboot:

```
# sysctl -p
```

Setting file descriptors

Editing the number of file descriptors on the Linux system can help a directory server access files more efficiently, so we will start by looking at the current setting:

```
# cat /proc/sys/fs/file-max
```

If the value is less than 64,000, then increase the limit in the /etc/sysctl file:

```
fs.file-max = 64000
```

Run the following command to read the new value we have just set, saving a restart:

```
# sysctl -p
```

For this setting to be effective, we must also allow all users to be allowed to have enough open files. Edit the /etc/security/limits.conf file to include the following lines:

```
*    soft    nofiles    8192
*    hard    nofiles    8192
```

This allows all users (*) to have a maximum of 8,192 open files (nofiles). We set both limits to the same value, but the soft limit can be exceeded with just a warning, while the hard limit cannot be exceeded.

Creating the directory server user and group

When configuring the directory, we will need to assign the service a user and group ID; the default is the `nobody` account, but we should create a non-privileged user and group dedicated to the directory as follows:

```
# useradd -m ldap389
```

The `useradd` command will create the `ldap389` user and group.

At this stage, it is pertinent to reboot the system to ensure that the settings are in place before we start the installation of the directory server. With this in place, we can further prepare for the installation.

The EPEL repository

We will need to implement the EPEL repository. Using the `wget` command, you can download the RPM file that will configure the repository for you:

```
$ wget http://epel.mirror.net.in/epel/6/i386/epel-release-6-8.noarch.rpm
```

Once you have downloaded, install the RPM as root. This will create the repository file for you. The output of the `yum repolist` command should show the EPEL repository. The following screenshot is from my demonstration system:

```
[root@ldap1 ~]# yum repolist
Loaded plugins: fastestmirror, refresh-packagekit, security
Loading mirror speeds from cached hostfile
 * base: www.mirrorservice.org
 * epel: ftp.nluug.nl
 * extras: centos.hyve.com
 * updates: mirror.sov.uk.goscomb.net
repo id           repo name
base              CentOS-6 - Base
c6-local          CentOS-6 - Media
epel              Extra Packages for Enterprise Linux 6 - x86_64
extras            CentOS-6 - Extras
updates           CentOS-6 - Updates
```

Installing and configuring 389-ds

With the repository configured on our system, we are now ready to use `yum` to install the directory server:

```
# yum install -y 389-ds openldap-clients
```

Among other things, you will find that Java will be installed as there is a Java management console that simplifies connecting to and managing entries in the directory.

The configuration is made simple with the implementation of a script that will guide us through the configuration of the administration and directory services on CentOS. The administration service represents the LDAP server; the directory service itself represents an individual directory hosted on the administration server. A single administration server can look after directories for company A and company B. The two directories can be administered separately.

The setup is achieved by running the script, `setup-ds-admin.pl`. The script is installed in your PATH statement. The default is for the script to run interactively but, especially where servers are setup frequently, you may use an answer file to accompany the script.

Running the following command will configure the directory and administration services interactively:

```
# setup-ds-admin.pl
```

This command, when run, will lead you into a menu, which is explained as follows:

1. **Continue with setup**: Choose `yes` to continue with the script at the first prompt.

2. **dsktune**: The tuning analysis will be run to check that you have RAM greater than 1024 MB and that the other preflight checks are in place.

3. **Choose a setup type**:
   1. **Express**
   2. **Typical**
   3. **Custom**

   We will choose 2 for **Typical**.

4. **Set the computer name**: Next, we set the computer name. This should be default to your hostname; in my case `ldap1.tup.com`.

5. **Set the user which the directory server will run**: This we set to `ldap389` in our case, the dedicated user we created.

6. **Set the group which the directory server will run**: We will use the `ldap389` group.

7. **Register the new directory server with an existing server**: We will choose `No` as this is the first server. If another server pre-existed, we could register this installation with that server.

8. **Give the configuration directory server a user ID and password**: We can accept the preset name of the admin. We use this account to log in to the directory server.

9. **The configuration directory server domain**: The domain I am using is tup.com. We will create an LDAP domain to reflect this.

10. **Set the directory server port**: The default port for LDAP is 389, and we will keep this as the default.

11. **Set the directory server identifier**: We will then be prompted for a unique name for the server in the directory. This will default to the first part of the hostname, in my case, ldap1.

12. **Set the directory suffix**: LDAP names are comma separated. The LDAP suffix will now be displayed similar to the following and will make up the top container in the LDAP tree:

    ○   dc=tup, dc=com

13. **Set the directory manager ID**: This is the LDAP directory manager and has a default name of cn=Directory Manager. We will need to set a secure password for this.

14. **Set the administration server port**: The administration port can be used to manage the server through the Java console. We will leave the default port at 9830.

The interactive setup is now complete, and the configuration will be created along with the default entries. The service should start in the final stage and a success message will be shown. We should ensure that the services start correctly on boot using chkconfig:

```
# chkconfig dirsrv on
# chkconfig dirsrv-admin on
```

 Remember that dirsrv runs on port 389 and is the LDAP directory. The dirsrv-admin is the administration server that listens on port 9830

Testing the installation

Congratulations! You now have an LDAP server, and we can test the configuration in a couple of ways. Firstly, we can use the `ldapsearch` command to display entries from the directory, and then we will use the 389-console, the GUI tool that we can manage LDAP with. In the following command, the `-x` option is for simple authentication and the `-b` option is the search base:

```
$ ldapsearch -x -b dc=tup,dc=com
```

The output from this will list, in **Lightweight Directory Interchange Format (LDIF)**, some containers and groups that were created during the configuration. The following screenshot shows one such group from the output on my system:

```
# HR Managers, Groups, tup.com
dn: cn=HR Managers,ou=Groups,dc=tup,dc=com
objectClass: top
objectClass: groupOfUniqueNames
cn: HR Managers
ou: groups
description: People who can manage HR entries
uniqueMember: cn=Directory Manager
```

The big advantage that we have with the 389-ds is the GUI. We can run it from the server or we could install the console on a client machine. We will run it from the server using the following command:

```
$ 389-console -a http://ldap1.tup.com:9830
```

We will be presented with a graphical console, as shown in the following screenshot, in which we can log in as an admin:

LDAP user account management

The purpose of the directory is to house user accounts. These accounts do not have to be used for authentication but we can use them for authentication. This may be for other CentOS or Linux systems as well as services such as Apache. We will now look at creating user accounts in the directory both from the command line and from the GUI console. If we start with the GUI console, we can create and export the user and reimport it from the command line.

Adding users using the GUI console

We can log in to the console using the admin account as before. From the main welcome page, we should choose the **Users and Groups** tab and then, select the **Search** button. With nothing in the search dialog, the search will return all users, groups and containers. The container objects that we can see are organizational units; an **organizational unit (OU)** is a little like a folder within a filesystem. In the directory, OUs are used to organize objects. Navigating to the OU named "people", we can use the menu to **Create | User**, (found at the bottom of the screen). This will open a form for use to complete the user's details. On the user form, we will add the following data:

First Name	Bob
Last Name	Bloggs
Common Name	Bob Bloggs
User ID	bbloggs (it is suggested to keep it all lowercase)
Password	Password1
Confirm Password	Password1

If we only needed a user to support an application login, such as from an Apache web server, this is all we would need. As we ultimately would like to log in from Linux, we will also complete the **Posix User** form as follows:

- **Enable Posix User Attributes**: Selected
- **UID Number**: 5000
- **GID Number**: 100
- **Home Directory**: /home/bbloggs
- **Login Shell**: /bin/bash

These attributes then combine to create our user. This will be displayed in the 389-console as well as in `ldapsearch`. If we rerun the earlier search, this time, we will add a filter to display only those objects that match `posixAccount`:

```
$ ldapsearch -x -b dc=tup,dc=com objectClass=posixAccount
```

This should just show a single entry.

Adding users from the command line

To create users from the command line, we have a similar tool to `ldapsearch`. The `ldapadd` command will create users in the directory. The user account details will be defined within an LDIF file to use as an argument to the `ldapadd` command. We will additionally need to be authenticated to perform this operation as anonymous connections, because as you will imagine, it cannot create entries within the directory. We will begin by ensuring the authentication is correct by using `ldapsearch`; this will also allow us to view all attributes for the new user `bbloggs`. We will use this output, once edited, to create a new user when imported with `ldapadd`

```
$ ldapsearch -x -D "cn=directory manager" -w Password1 -b dc=tup,dc=com
objectClass=posixAccount > /tmp/user.ldif
```

Using this search, we now authenticate as the directory manager and redirect the output through to the `/tmp/user.ldif` file. Using the `-W` option in place of `-w` will allow the password to be requested during the operation rather than being placed on the command line.

We should edit the file using your preferred text editor so that it looks similar to the following:

```
dn: uid=ssmith,ou=People,dc=tup,dc=com
givenName: Sally
sn: Smith
loginShell: /bin/bash
uidNumber: 5001
gidNumber: 100
objectClass: top
objectClass: person
objectClass: organizationalPerson
objectClass: inetorgperson
objectClass: posixAccount
uid: ssmith
cn: Sally Smith
homeDirectory: /home/ssmith
userPassword: Password1
```

We are setting the uidNumber manually, and it must be incremented along with changing the other name-based fields.

Once the file is edited, we can create the user from the command line using the ldapadd command:

```
$ ldapadd -x -D "cn=directory manager" -w Password1 -f /tmp/user.ldif
```

If you typed correctly, then you should see a success message similar to the following screenshot taken from my system:

```
[root@ldap1 ~]# ldapadd -x -D "cn=directory manager" -w Password1  -f user.ldif
adding new entry "uid=ssmith,ou=People,dc=tup,dc=com"
```

The password for the new user will be stored in an encrypted form, although we add it in clear text from the LDIF file.

We have now seen how we can use the standard OpenLDAP tool to search and add entries to our directory as well as the comfort of being able to use the GUI tools if we prefer. We have two users in the system now that can be provisioned to client Linux systems.

LDAP authentication

We will use an additional CentOS 6.5 server on which we will configure the OpenLDAP client for authentication so that we make use of the central account database that we established on the 389-ds server.

From the client machine, we will need to install the following packages:

- openldap
- openldap-client
- nss-pam-ldapd

This will be managed through the standard yum repositories:

```
# yum install openldap openldap-clients  nss-pam-ldapd
```

Once this is installed, we will make one change to the `/etc/sysconfig/authconfig` file. We will edit the line that reads `FORCELEGACY=no` to read `FORCELEGACY=yes`. This change will allow us to use LDAP rather than LDAPS. Although it would be more secure to use LDAPS as the information encrypts data exchange, using LDAP, we alleviate the need to create certificates for the server, which is adequate on a local network.

To configure the authentication, we can use the `authconfig` command:

```
# authconfig --enableldap --enableldapauth --enablemkhomedir \
--enablemkhomedir --ldapserver=ldap://192.168.0.76:389/ \
--ldapbasedn="dc=tup,dc=com" \
--enablecache -- disablefingerprint --update
```

This configures authentication and will write the configuration to the correct files. You will notice that we include the option to create user home directories, `--enablemkhomedir`; on login, if a user's home directory does not exist, it will be created. We added the home directory path when creating the users, but this will not have created the home directory. These home directories are not shared unless we remap the `/home` directory on client machines to a central location.

We can verify the configuration now using the `getent` command we touched upon in the previous chapter:

```
# getent passwd
```

This should list the `bbloggs` and `ssmith` account from the central LDAP server. This can be seen in the output on my system:

```
bblogs:*:5000:100:Bob Bloggs:/home/bblogs:/bin/bash
ssmith:*:5001:100:Sally Smith:/home/ssmith:/bin/bash
```

We can now log out and log in again as one of our users. Choosing the `ssmith` account, we log in to the graphical gnome desktop, navigate to the **System | Preferences**, and select the **About Me** button. We can see that we are logged in as **Sally**. The output from my system is shown in the following screenshot:

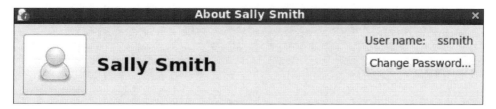

Summary

In this chapter, we introduced you to the concept of identity management and showed the use of the 389-ds, the enriched OpenLDAP server on CentOS. It is enriched with a simplified setup script and graphical tools; however, we also saw how we can use traditional OpenLDAP tools to create and search entries in a directory. We finished the chapter by allowing a second CentOS server to use the account database shared by 389-ds supplying us with a single logon across many systems.

In the next chapter, we will discuss the Nginx web server, the new kid on the block, but a refreshing alternative to Apache.

8
Nginx – Deploying a Performance-centric Web Server

When it comes to web servers, it seems that Apache gets all the attention, and you may be led to believe that there is little competition; so let me introduce Nginx to you. We have seen many articles implementing the **Linux Apache MySQL and PHP (LAMP)** technology. We shall play this a little left field and look at **Linux Nginx MySQL and PHP (LEMP)**; the E in LEMP comes from the phonetic version of the web server that is pronounced *engine-x*, allowing us to place a well needed vowel to create the acronym LEMP. The web server was first introduced in 2004, and Nginx is beginning to make inroads into the enterprise web space, being faster to deliver web content than equivalent Apache servers.

The following topics are going to be covered in this chapter:

- **Installing and configuring Nginx**: We will install and configure the Nginx web server
- **Installing PHP**: We will install PHP5 to integrate with Nginx
- **Installing MySQL**: We will install and configure the MySQL database server
- **Creating dynamic web content**: Using the LEMP stack, we will learn to create simple dynamic web pages

Installing and configuring Nginx

To begin this chapter, we will need to install the web server Nginx on our CentOS system. Nginx is the new kid on the block in terms of web servers, but in recent surveys from NetCraft, `http://www.netcraft.com`, we have seen that the Internet has fallen a little out of love with Apache, with Nginx making steady rises since its introduction in 2004. That said, in May 2014, Apache still had 37 percent of the web server share with Microsoft at 33 percent and Nginx at 14 percent.

Installing Nginx

Nginx is not part of the standard repositories, but we can use the EPEL repository that we used to install the 389-ds we looked at in *Chapter 7, LDAP – A Better Type of User*. With the **Extra Packages for Enterprise Linux (EPEL)** repository in place, we can install using yum, and then once we have Nginx installed, we can start the service and configure it with `chkconfig` to start on the system boot:

```
# yum install nginx
# service nginx start
# chkconfig nginx on
```

There is a welcome page configured in the default site's configuration that points to `/usr/share/nginx/html/`. We will leave this in place, but will create our own document root soon. We can test the functionality of the web server by browsing to the site `http://localhost` as seen in the following screenshot:

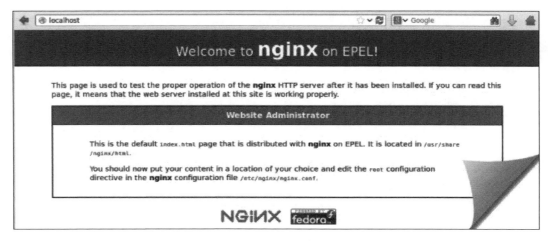

That was really quite easy, wasn't it! We probably need to replace this web page with one of our own and tidy up some other configurations; but this simple test is good enough to prove the site is up and running.

Configuring Nginx

The configuration directory for Nginx, or what is referred to as `ServerRoot`, is `/etc/nginx`. The main configuration file is `/etc/nginx/nginx.conf`; however, the web server takes a very modular approach to its configuration, and there is an include statement within the main configuration file that will reference all `.conf` files in `conf.d`. The statement from the `nginx.conf` reads as follows:

```
include /etc/nginx/conf.d/*.conf
```

In this way, it is easy to add in additional configurations without having to edit existing files and risking costly errors. The default configuration that defines the initial server is `/etc/nginx/conf.d/default.conf`. To help understand a little of the anatomy of the Nginx configurations files, let's take a look at the following diagram:

To gain the best understanding of the configuration of Nginx, it is often better to start with your own configuration. Start with something simple and add to it. To this end, we will rename `default.conf` to something else and create our own configuration. For a simple server configuration, we need little more than five lines of code:

```
server {
    listen 80;
    root /var/www/html;
    index index.html;
}
```

The previous lines can save this configuration to the new file, `/etc/nginx/conf.d/main.conf`. We will then rename the original configuration `/etc/nginx/conf.d/default.conf` to `/etc/nginx/conf.d/default.conf.old`. It is only `.conf` files that are included so in this way, we can maintain the original configuration without effecting the operation of the web server.

The new configuration that we have is very simple and sparse, and we can explain the limited directives:

- `listen`: We will listen on all interfaces to TCP port 80.
- `root`: Here we set the document root to `/var/www/html`. It is better to have variable content like this in the `/var` structure rather than the default location of `/usr`.
- `index`: We set the default page, often known as the welcome page, to `index.html`. If the URL from the client is entered using the server name only or server name with a directory path without specifying a web page, then the server will look for a page named `index.html`.

We will need to create the directory structure for the document root and fashion a simple web page:

```
# mkdir /var/www/html

#echo '<h1>Welcome to NGINX</h1>' > /var/www/html/index.html
```

In an ideal world, before restarting the Nginx server, we should endeavor to test any configuration changes. In this way, we can avoid the embarrassing issue where the restart of the server is interrupted by configuration anomalies. When we issue a restart to the service, we will need to first stop and then start Nginx. Stopping the service will not be a problem, but the start might be if we have omitted a semi-colon or other little typo. Consequently, it may be few minutes before we can identify the problem and resume normal service. Having made any changes to the Nginx configuration, we should always test the integrity of these edits before restarting. Using the `/usr/sbin/nginx -t` command, we can perform this check and ensure that if we stop the server, we will be able to start it again. If you prefer, the same test is available by the use of the `service nginx configtest` command.

Other options to the `nginx` command include `-v` for the version of Nginx and `-V` to show the version and configuration options. If we do come across errors, we can check the logfile `/var/log/nginx/error.log`. The `tail` command is often good for this since only the last 10 lines will be shown. The path to the error log is configured in the `/etc/nginx/nginx.conf` with the following line:

```
error_log /var/log/nginx/error.log
```

If required, you could change this to a different logfile; but the default seems reasonable. For now, we can satisfy ourselves that the configuration is OK and restart the service as follows:

```
# nginx -t && service nginx restart
```

In this command sequence, the `&&` operator ensures that the restart will only occur if the first command succeeds and the configuration check gave no errors.

We can revisit our site now. It may appear a little less glamorous, but it is all our own work as we can see in the following screenshot:

Configuring a 404 Document Not Found Error page

Another small change we will implement is to control the page not found or HTTP 404 errors. If a user types a page that does not exist, then they will be displayed a very simple error page. We can customize this a little and, at least, give the user a link back to the main index page. If we reedit the configuration file, `/etc/nginx/conf.d/main.conf` it will now read:

```
server {
    listen 80;
    root /var/www/html;
    index index.html;
    error_page 404 not_found.html;
}
```

The extra line `error_page` looks for HTTP 404 errors and returns the page `not_found.html`. We, of course, need to create the page, and it could look similar to this, as a very simple example providing the error and a link to return to the index page:

```
<h2>We could not locate the document</h2>
<a href='/index.html'>Home</a>
```

Remember to test the configuration; we can restart the web server as follows:

```
# nginx -t && service nginx restart
```

Then, access a page that we know does not exist, such as `http://localhost/page1.html`. We should see the new error page, which may look like this if you used my example:

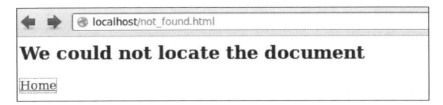

Although the design of the web page is simple and bare, we are not trying to teach HTML or CSS tricks here, but more about gaining the idea of how we can use directives in Nginx to issue our own custom error pages.

Installing PHP

Now that we have the web server up and running, we can add the PHP processor that we need to be able to add PHP elements to our page and subsequently create dynamic web content. Nginx uses the PHP FastCGI Process Manager, which is again available from the EPEL repository. We have that set up already from the Nginx install and the earlier install of 389-ds. To install PHP and the PHP-FPM, we can use yum:

```
# yum install php-fpm
```

Once installed, we need to edit the FPM so that it uses the correct accounts for Nginx. To do this, we can edit `/etc/php-fpm.d/www.conf`. We will need to edit the user and group lines from apache to nginx:

```
user = nginx
group = nginx
```

We also need to make sure that the Nginx web server knows to forward PHP files to the FPM service on port 9000. We can re-edit `/etc/nginx/conf.d/main.conf` and add it to the server section:

```
server {
 listen 80;
 root /var/www/html;
 index index.html;
 error_page 404 not_found.html;
 location ~ \.php$ {
  fastcgi_pass 127.0.0.1:9000;
  fastcgi_index index.php;
```

```
    fastcgi_param SCRIPT_FILENAME $document_root$fastcgi_script_name
    include fastcgi_params;
  }


}
```

The code we add is all within the original server block. The file will end correctly with two right braces. We are closing the new location block and the original server code block. Taking stock of the edit, we can see that we have defined a `location` block. This is used when we access a web page that ends with `.php` or, more simply, a PHP page. The definition for the location block looks a little akin to comic book profanities, and that should identify for you that it is in fact a regular expression; the tilde (~) denotes that we look for a regular expression match. The expression we search for is URLs that end in `.php`. The `$` symbol denotes the end of the string. The complete expression starts with the escape character `\`; this is needed as the period (dot) has special meaning in regular expressions. To protect this, we use `\` to inform Nginx to read it as literal dot rather than as a regular expression language element. The rest of the code block then denotes that we should pass the PHP code through to the PHP interpreter by means of port 9000 on the local host. The `include` statement reads in a preconfigured file for PHP to set various parameter values.

We can now test and restart the Nginx web server and start the FPM service, configuring it for autostart:

```
# nginx -t && service nginx restart
# service php-fpm start
# chkconfig php-fpm on
```

With a little luck and a following wind, all has been successful, but of course, we do need to test a PHP page now; this can be easily achieved by calling a simple `phpinfo()` function. This is a really simple test that will prove PHP is up and running on your CentOS system. We will return to the Nginx document root directory, `/var/www/html` and create a new page, `info.php`. The PHP extension is important as this is what we look for in the location block: to direct through to the PHP interpreter. The page that we will create could not be any more simple; however, the power behind the function will display a lot in your web browser for very little typing. We can mix HTML code and PHP code in the single file, but we will just use only PHP here. The PHP block starts with `<?php` and ends with the closing tag, `?>`. Each line of PHP code ends with a semi-colon. The `/var/www/html/ info.php` file will look like this when edited:

```
<?php
    phpinfo();
?>
```

When we direct the browser to the page with `http://127.0.0.1/info.php`, we should be encouraged with a comprehensive page detailing the configuration of PHP on our CentOS host. See the output from my system in the following screenshot:

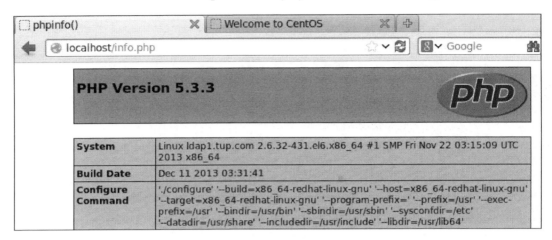

Very quickly we have been able to demonstrate the power that lies behind PHP with this simple test. We also can be confident that we have configured PHP correctly with Nginx on our system. We will now add the MySQL database.

Installing MySQL

MySQL is the open source database solution now managed by Oracle, and of course this is a pivotal component of the LEMP stack that we are implementing. The MySQL server can store data to be displayed later on our web pages. We will communicate from Nginx using PHP with the database server. We can use `yum` to install MySQL and the PHP modules:

```
# yum install php-mysql mysql-server
# service mysqld start
# chkconfig mysqld on
```

Once MySQL is installed, we need to secure the installation a little further; even if it is only to set the MySQL root password. Out of the box security in many systems tends to be a little light. Using the `mysql_secure_installation` command, we can add a little extra security. Running the program will lead you into a simple interactive prompted session:

```
# mysql_secure_installation
```

The resulting wizard will prompt you through the process described in the following:

- **Enter current password for root**: This is currently blank, so just use the *Enter* key.
- **Set root password**: We will choose Y.
- **New Password**: Enter the new password twice.
- **Remove anonymous users**: Choose Y for this. In this way, only configured accounts have access.
- **Disallow root login remotely**: This is usually a good idea, preventing remote MySQL root access. We only need access from this host, so we will answer Y.
- **Remove test database and access to it**: There is a database test that is empty. If we do not need it, we should delete it.
- **Reload privilege table now**: We will answer Y to make these settings effective.

If for nothing else, this is one of the simplest ways to set the MySQL root account password and remind us to verify other settings as we run through the simple script. When we are ready, we can test the operation of the database server from the Linux command line:

```
$ mysql -u root -p -e 'show databases;'
```

We are authenticating as root and will be prompted for the password we set earlier. The -e option allows us to execute a MySQL query directly from the command line, and the subsequent query we issue will list all databases. Of course, these will be system databases, as we have not created our own. We can use this same query within a web page to show that we have connectivity to the database from Nginx later. From the query results, we should see two databases listed: information_schema and mysql.

Create dynamic web content

To demonstrate how easily we can create dynamic web pages that will connect to the database using PHP from the Nginx server, we will create a new PHP page in /var/www/html. So fire up your favorite editor, and we will create the page within the document root, /var/www/html/db.php:

```
<h2>Databases</h2>
<?php
    $dbh=mysqli_connect("localhost","root","Password1");
    $result=mysqli_query($dbh, "SHOW DATABASES");
    while ($row = mysqli_fetch_assoc($result)) {
      echo $row['Database'] . "<BR>";
    }
?>
```

The code again is kept as simple as possible, and ideally we would include the connection credentials stored within another file that was not accessible to the web server, allowing access only from the PHP process; however, keeping the code to a minimum does aide the learning process at this early stage.

In this PHP file, you can see that we mix a little HTML code with the PHP code, starting with heading tags before entering into the PHP block. The PHP code first connects to the MySQL server, and then we execute the same query we demonstrated before, from the command line. Before we test this, we will need to restart Nginx and the `php-fpm` service:

```
# service nginx restart
# service php-fpm restart
```

This time, the results will show in the web browser and illustrating that we have a simple dynamic page created from database content. At this stage, we can be happy that we have a LEMP server up and running. With this proof of concept in place, we can now consider building further projects on the LEMP stack, and I certainly hope that you can take a little enthusiasm away with you to read a little more on what you can achieve with PHP and MySQL.

This is the home page that you'll be seeing:

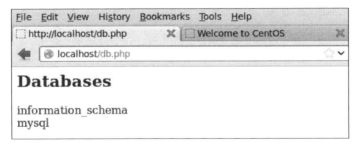

Summary

In this chapter, we have seen how we can build upon the CentOS host and the LEMP stack and implementing Nginx, MySQL, and PHP. Nginx is quite simple to configure but provides faster access to web content than Apache, but can equally be configured to communicate with PHP and MySQL in the backend. Gaining the basic knowledge of configuring PHP and MySQL to operate with the web server can build the grounding you need to develop your web application further.

In the following chapter, we will see how to implement Puppet on CentOS as a central configuration server to allow configuration changes to be made on one server to replicate to other configured clients.

9
Puppet – Now You Are the Puppet Master

Puppet from Puppet Labs allows for central administration of your Linux devices. The central Puppet server is known as the Puppet master, continuing the analogy with puppetry. This master device certainly allows you to control servers and desktops (nodes in Puppet terms) from a single device, albeit not in the marionette style with pieces of a string. The Puppet master specifies the desired state to each node, and every 30 minutes, the node connects to the Puppet master and sends facts about its resources; if it does not meet the desired state, then the node will fix itself to meet it. During the course of this chapter, we will investigate the Puppet configuration including:

- **Installing the Puppet master**: We will install and configure the Puppet master from the Puppet Labs repository. The Puppet master will act as the central configuration server and store the desired configuration state for each node.

- **Puppet resource**: We will use the `puppet resource` command to manually manage resources on the node. Resources represent the fundamental building blocks of a desired state and can include files, users, services, cron jobs, and software packages on the node.

- **Managing packages, services, and files**: These three resources represent the main trifecta in Puppet management, and if we can manage these, we can pretty much manage the node. We will create the resource declarations in manifest files and test them on local and remote puppet agents.

Installing the Puppet master

As we know with many services that have to be installed on CentOS, we have to make sure that the plumbing is correct before we start. The plumbing, in the case of the Puppet master, means:

- TCP port 8140 must be open through the firewall
- The Puppet master should be resolvable by the hostname puppet by DNS or local hosts files
- Time should be synchronized
- A configured Puppet Labs yum repository

I've detailed these in the following sections.

Configuring the firewall

I am not using a host-based firewall in the demonstration machine. This may not be the case on your systems, and if you are using a firewall, you will need to allow TCP port 8140 through the INPUT chain. The status of the firewall can be checked with the following command:

```
# iptables -L
```

This will list the rules that are in place and the default policy. If there are no rules in place and the default policy is ACCEPT, then you will not have firewall-related issues, and you can relax.

DNS

Puppet agents are running on each client or node and will try and communicate with the Puppet master using the default hostname, puppet. This can be changed in the /etc/puppet.conf file. This change will need to be implemented on each agent so it is often the easiest way to create an ADDRESS record or CNAME record in the local DNS, which can resolve the host puppet to the IP address of your desired Puppet master host. In the demonstration lab, I have the correct CNAME record in place. Using the ping command, we can see that the hostname is resolvable, and the output is shown in the following screenshot:

```
[root@ldap1 init.d]# ping puppet
PING ldap1.tup.com (192.168.0.76) 56(84) bytes of data.
64 bytes from 192.168.0.76: icmp_seq=1 ttl=64 time=0.042 ms
64 bytes from 192.168.0.76: icmp_seq=2 ttl=64 time=0.036 ms
64 bytes from 192.168.0.76: icmp_seq=3 ttl=64 time=0.036 ms
64 bytes from 192.168.0.76: icmp_seq=4 ttl=64 time=0.036 ms
64 bytes from 192.168.0.76: icmp_seq=5 ttl=64 time=0.035 ms
```

Network Time Protocol

If you have not already configured the time on your Puppet master server and agent nodes, then you should do so using the **Network Time Protocol** (**NTP**). This will ensure that they all share the same accurate time. Accurate time is required across all devices, as the Puppet master will act as a certificate server issuing certificates to trusted nodes, and the timestamp on the certificate cannot be in the future. In setting up NTP on the Puppet master, we will first synchronize the time to an NTP server and then configure regular time updates using NTP and entries stored within the /etc/ntp.conf file, as follows:

```
# ntpdate uk.pool.ntp.org
```

The previous command does a single, one-off update with a UK-based NTP server. This sets the time so that regular updates may take place. If this is not set, then it is possible that the time will not be synchronized as the NTP client must be within 1,000 seconds of the NTP server for regular updates to take place. We can now start the NTP service and configure it for autostart. If we do not make any changes to the configuration file, /etc/ntp.conf, then time will synchronize with servers from the NTP pool. If you have a local time server already up and running on your network, then it will be worthwhile to use that device as the time source as follows:

```
# service ntpd start
# chkconfig ntpd on
```

The Puppet lab repository

The Puppet master is not available in the standard CentOS repositories, nor unfortunately, the EPEL repositories, which we have already configured. This requires us to add the Puppet Labs software repositories. These repositories will provide the latest Puppet agent and master software. The Puppet agent is required on all nodes and the master software on the server. We will create the YUM repository for Puppet directly by installing the RPM from a web URL. The RPM will define only the repository file in /etc/yum.repos.d.

```
#  rpm -ivh http://yum.puppetlabs.com/puppetlabs-release-el-6.noarch.rpm
```

This will complete quickly, as the only file that it needs to create is the repository definition. With the repository set, we are now ready to install the Puppet master. The following command will install the Puppet master and agent to the latest version available from the Puppet Labs repositories:

```
# yum install puppet-server
```

As always, we should start the service and enable it for autostart. When this is done, we can use the `netstat` command to show that the Puppet master is listening on the TCP port `8140`:

```
# service puppetmaster start
# chkconfig puppetmaster on
# netstat -antl | grep :8140
```

Puppet resource

Versions of Puppet from 2.6 and later (the current release is 3.6) use the single binary puppet with subcommands for specific tasks. The earlier version had separate binaries for all of the subcommands. In the previous set of commands, we used the traditional CentOS syntax to start the Puppet master and then to enable the service for autostart; we could achieve the same result using the `/usr/bin/puppet` command along with the `resource` subcommand:

```
# puppet resource Service puppetmaster enable=true ensure=running
```

With this command, we direct our attention to the `puppetmaster` service, enable it for autostart (`enable=true`), and start it if required (`ensure=running`). This represents the very essence of how Puppet works. Of course, to manage many clients, we will create manifest files with similar resource rules to enforce the desired state. In itself though, we will configure the desired state of the node with the use of the `puppet resource` command.

Along with setting the desired state, we can view the state of all services or a single named service using very similar commands; the following are two such commands; the first command will display all services, and the second command will display only the `puppetmaster` service:

```
# puppet resource Service
# puppet resource Service puppetmaster
```

The output from the command specific to the `puppetmaster` service is shown in the following screen capture:

```
[root@ldap1 init.d]# puppet resource Service puppetmaster
service { 'puppetmaster':
  ensure => 'running',
  enable => 'true',
}
```

As mentioned earlier in the introduction to this chapter, the three main resources that we manage with Puppet include:

*   Service
*   Files
*   Packages

Along with these main resources, we have others, which include the following:

*   Users
*   Groups
*   Cron jobs
*   Notify
*   Yumrepo
*   ssh_authorized_key
*   Interface

To gain an understanding of how Puppet can manage these resources, we will work through an example using the `puppet resource` command to manually enforce a desired state on our node. Even though the node on which we run the command is the Puppet master, for all intents and purposes, we will only use the client, which is the Puppet agent at this stage. The example we used earlier with puppet resource demonstrates what can be achieved with Puppet before moving the desired state configuration into manifest files on the Puppet master.

Using puppet resource user, we can ensure that a user account is present on a system, by referencing an account that does not exist, Puppet will create the account and set the given attribute's password. If we need to delete an account, we can use the `ensure=>absent` attribute.

To begin, we must obtain the encrypted password for the new user account. There are different mechanisms that can be used to do this, but here I will use Python from the command line to generate the password:

```
# python -c 'import crypt; print crypt.crypt("Password1","$5$RA")'
```

The output from this command will be the SHA-256 password to be used by the new user. We are now ready to use Puppet to create the user:

```
# puppet resource User newuser ensure=present uid='2222'
gid='100' home='/home/newuser' managehome=true shell='/bin/bash'
password='<encrypted password>'
```

Blocks of code like these that describe the resource are known as **resource declarations**.

This will create the user with the set of desired attribute values. The home directory for the user will be created along with the user account. This behavior is controlled with the managehome attribute; setting this to be true will create the directory.

Although we would not want this set manually on all servers, as in this case, we could use a similar method to allow periodic password changes for the root account across all nodes as well as ensure other system accounts exist.

Managing packages, services, and files

We will move on from this manual configuration and become familiar with Puppet as a central configuration server, whereby we can define settings within manifest files that will be distributed to the required nodes. To begin this, we will create the manifest file; these are just text files, and apply it locally on the Puppet master using puppet apply. Once we have verified that the manifest is working and enforcing the desired state, we will enlist the clients and see true Puppet automation at work.

The building blocks for Puppet start with the resource declarations that we have already looked at. These declarations are written to manifest files, which have the extension .pp. Within the manifest file, resources can be grouped together into classes. A class often represents related resources, such as the openssh-server package, the sshd service, and the /etc/ssh/sshd_config configuration file. It would seem reasonable to group these resources together in a class definition.

We can view these building blocks by taking a look inside an example manifest file, as shown in the following diagram:

```
example.pp

    class ssh{

              file {'/etc/motd':
                        content=> 'Welcome to the Tup.com'
              }
              service {'ssh':
                        enable=> true,
                        ensure=> running,

              }

    }

    include ssh
```

Classes

Classes are reusable because a class can be used by multiple node definitions and are said to be singleton in the sense that once a given class is used on a node, it can only be used once and cannot be redeclared for that node. The class we have created here is named ssh. A class has to be first defined and then declared. The following code block is an example of a class definition:

```
class web-servers {
   code......
}
```

The following example code shows the same class being declared:

```
include web-servers
```

Resource definition

Resource definitions, such as what we looked at earlier for the user resource, do not need to be enclosed within classes; however, related resources are often grouped together by means of the class for ease of assignment to nodes. In this example, we define a file resource and a service resource. The name of the service resource must match the name of the service on the node to which it will be assigned; in the case of CentOS, the OpenSSH server is the sshd service.

A resource in Puppet is an instance of a specific resource type. To list all the available types in CentOS, we can use the describe subcommand:

```
# puppet describe -l
```

A resource type has a defined schema that states which attributes are available. To list the schema details of a resource type, we can use the describe subcommand again:

```
# puppet describe -s User
# puppet describe User
```

A short description is shown with and without the -s option; a full listing of the resource type schema is listed. In the previous commands, we display information for the user resource type.

Earlier in this chapter, we created a new user account from the command line using puppet resource. If we needed a system account on many nodes and wished that Puppet provision the account, we can create a user resource definition within a manifest file similar to the following:

```
user { 'puppetuser' :
  ensure => present,
  uid => '99',
  gid => '99',
  shell => '/bin/false',
  password => '$5$RA$e7cMcsFNqvFkZrlm62fnzy0vpN2GxrOjzpsLaVQzIc4',
  home => '/tmp',
  managehome => false,
}
```

Puppet facts

In the example manifest we listed earlier, we defined a file resource for the /etc/motd file. This is displayed when a user logs into the system, be it locally or via a remote SSH connection. The Puppet agent will compare facts from the node's configuration to see if it matches the desired state. These facts are gathered from the machine's configuration using the /usr/bin/facter command. We can display these facts in the following way:

```
$ facter
```

The preceding command will display all the facts, whereas the following command will display just the IP address:

```
$ facter ipaddress
```

We can further expand the resource definition using additional attributes for the file and fill out the content with some facts as follows:

```
file {'/etc/motd' :
  ensure => file,
  mode => 0644,
  content => "Welcome to TUP
This is a ${operatingsystem}  ${operatingsystemrelease} host with IP
${ipaddress}
",
}
```

If this resource definition was applied to a node, it would ensure that the file is of the type "file"; rather than a directory, the permission would be set to rw- r-- r--, and the contents would expand with three variables created from facts. This will create contents similar to the following screenshot:

```
cat /etc/motd
Welcome to TUP
This is a CentOS 6.5 host with IP 192.168.0.76
[root@ldap1 motd]#
```

Remember that we only need to create the resource definition once. On the Puppet server, this one definition will then be applied to all the nodes it is assigned to. However, using variables based on facts from each node, we can create unique content for each individual /etc/motd file.

Using include

The include statement declares the use of the class. If we define a class and do not use the include statement, then none of the resource definitions will be used. The class can be defined within the same manifest in which it is declared, but more often, classes are defined in separate manifest files created within the puppet module path. The modulepath defaults to the /etc/puppet/modules and /usr/share/puppet/modules directories. You can view the module path, which is colon delimited, using the following command:

```
# puppet config print modulepath
```

The output from my CentOS system shows the default settings, as shown in the following screen capture:

```
[root@ldap1 puppet]# puppet config print modulepath
/etc/puppet/modules:/usr/share/puppet/modules
[root@ldap1 puppet]#
```

Creating and testing manifests

Manifests are ASCII text files that have the `.pp` extension. These files contain class declarations and/or resource definitions. Classes are also defined and declared within manifests; however, as mentioned before, they are often defined in separate manifest files to those where they are declared. This allows for greater modularity of your code. The manifest file can be supplied as a local file and invoked via the `apply` subcommand of Puppet or, more often, from the Puppet master. We will apply the manifest locally using `puppet apply`. The file that we will create will be consistent with a client server deployment so that we can reuse the same file once we have tested it locally; for this, we will create the file as `/etc/puppet/manifests/site.pp`. Nodes, when connecting to the Puppet master, will look for the `site.pp` file for their configuration. The example manifest is shown in the following code:

```
class tup {
  file {'/etc/motd' :
  ensure => file,
  mode => 0644,
  owner => 'root',
  group => 'root',
  content => "Welcome to TUP
This is a ${operatingsystem}  ${operatingsystemrelease} host with IP
${ipaddress}
",
  }
service {'sshd':
  ensure => running,
  enable => true,
  }
package { 'openssh-server' :
    ensure => installed,
  }
}
include tup
```

With the manifest created and saved under /etc/puppet/manifests/site.pp, we can validate the syntax of the file with the following command:

```
# puppet parser validate  /etc/puppet/manifests/site.pp
```

If errors can be seen, then we can re-edit the file to correct these errors, and when the output is error free, we can manually apply the file:

```
# puppet apply /etc/puppet/manifests/site.pp
```

Using the cat command, we can validate the contents of the /etc/motd file:

```
$ cat /etc/motd
```

If we now stop the sshd service and change the permissions of the file, we can see how Puppet ensures a consistent configuration:

```
# service sshd stop
# chmod 777 /etc/motd
```

With the changes made, we have diverged from the desired state and can now reapply the manifest; under normal client-server operations, the Puppet agent will check into the server every 30 minutes.

```
# puppet apply /etc/puppet/manifests/site.pp
```

The output should include notices similar to those in the following screenshot, indicating that the service has been started and the mode has been changed:

```
Notice: /Stage[main]/Tup/Service[sshd]/ensure: ensure changed 'stopped' to 'runn
ing'
Notice: /Stage[main]/Tup/File[/etc/motd]/mode: mode changed '0777' to '0644'
Notice: Finished catalog run in 0.95 seconds
[root@ldap1 manifests]#
```

Enrolling remote puppet agents

As we saw, Puppet can be effective in maintaining a consistent configuration, but we do not want to create the manifests on each device and run the puppet commands manually. To see the real strength of Puppet as a central configuration server, we need to enroll clients and have the puppet agent run as a service. As we mentioned before, the agent will check its desired state every 30 minutes automatically when the agent service is running.

From a remote CentOS 6.5 system, we will check whether we can resolve the hostname of the Puppet master, using the follow command line:

```
$ host puppet
```

As seen before, we will need to ensure that we have time synchronization on our remote node:

```
# ntpdate uk.pool.ntp.org
# service ntpd start
# chkconfig ntpd on
```

We will add the remote Puppet labs repository to the remote client CentOS system:

```
# rpm -ivh http://yum.puppetlabs.com/puppetlabs-release-el6.noarch.rpm
```

Finally, we will install the Puppet agent on the client system and display the version of Puppet:

```
# yum install puppet
# puppet --version
```

At the time of writing this, the version of the Puppet Labs repository is 3.6.2.

We are now ready to test the client. The first step towards this is to start the agent manually so that we can enroll the node on the server. This will submit a certificate signing request to the Puppet master, as the node is not yet enrolled:

```
# puppet agent test
```

Returning now to the console of the Puppet master, we can check the certificate authority for agent signing request:

```
# puppet ca list
```

We should see the request from the client machine on our lab setup; the client request shows centos65.tup.com. We can accept and sign this request using the following command:

```
 #  puppet ca --sign centos65.tup.com
```

We will now return to the client machine and rerun the test agent; this will download the signed certificate, and the agent will then download and apply the site.pp manifest:

```
# puppet agent test
```

We can now check the contents of the /etc/motd file. We should have the content we saw before, but with the IP address of this node. Using the cat command from the remote client machine, the output will look similar to the following screenshot:

```
[root@centos65 Desktop]# cat /etc/motd
Welcome to TUP
This is a CentOS 6.5 host with IP 192.168.0.123
[root@centos65 Desktop]# 
```

Now that we have installed the signed certificate onto the client, we can start the agent service and leave the system to manage itself; we can have even more time on the golf course now!

```
# service puppet start
# chkconfig puppet on
```

On CentOS, the agent service is just Puppet and with the service running, the agent will check the configuration every 30 minutes.

Summary

In this chapter, we looked at how we can implement central configuration management using Puppet. Although we only looked at it on CentOS, the configuration can work across many operating systems including Linux, Windows, and Unix. The main server is the Puppet master and agents connected on the TCP port 8140 to download the site manifest. This manifest can include other classes but will determine the desired configuration for a node.

As we move onto the next chapter, we will look at how we can use **pluggable authentication modules (PAM)** to help harden the CentOS host, as well as venture into the world of SELinux.

10
Security Central

Linux security is not a chapter in a book, it is a way of life. For every task that you carry out in CentOS, you should consider the security impact and how your actions can be made more secure. Of course, security takes many forms, and much of it is quite simple (for example, the physical security of servers locked in server rooms and so on. In this section, we will visit the world of **pluggable authentication modules (PAM)** and **SELinux**. Do not be scared of either, especially, SELinux; they are your friends. In this chapter, we will cover the following topics:

- **Understanding PAM configuration files**: At the heart of PAM are the files located in /etc/pam.d; I will lead you through their syntax and meaning
- **Limits of PAM**: Through PAM's limits module, we can restrict limits on system resources that can be obtained in a user session
- **SELinux**: This is a quick guide to SELinux, both through the filesystem and the user's perspective
- **Hardening Linux**: This is a checklist on what and how to secure your Linux server

Understanding PAM configuration files

Rather than building authentication into each and every application that needs it, most services in Linux will make use of modules such as PAM. These modules have the .so extension to identify them as standard modules, and are used by programs rather than the kernel directly. They make their home in /lib/security or /lib64/security, depending on whether your system is 32 bit or 64 bit. Each service or program that has PAM capabilities has its own configuration that dictates how authentication and session settings will be enforced; these files are located in /etc/pam.d. A quick look in this folder will reveal some recognizable names, such as sshd, sudo, su, and login, all representing services that have a level of authentication associated with them.

The /etc/pam.d/login file will be used by the console login program and /etc/ pamd/sshd by the OpenSSH server. There will be multiple lines in each configuration file, and every line will have settings for type, control, module-path, and optional arguments to the module.

From the following figure, you can gain some understanding of the file syntax and see the four type settings: account, auth, session, and password.

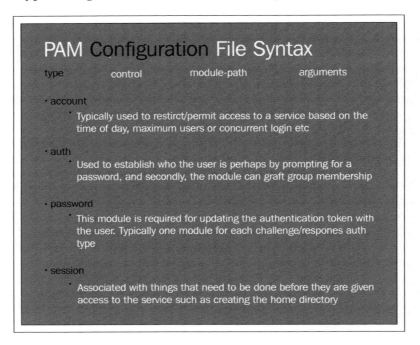

Take the following line as an example:

```
account   required   pam_nologin.so
```

This line has been taken from the /etc/pam.d/login file and has been set for the account type with the control set to required for the specified module: pam_nologin.so. This particular module checks for the existence of the /etc/ nologin file; if it does exist, then even on successful authentication the user will not gain access to the system. He or she will be shown either the contents of the / etc/nologin file or a generic message explaining that login could not occur. This approach in itself becomes a simple way to temporarily disable logins to a server by just creating the nologin file; delete the file to re-enable logins.

Each of the elements of a PAM configuration file are listed next.

Type

Type defines when the module will be invoked. There are 4 valid entries:

- **Account**: This is typically used to restrict or permit access to a service based on the time of day, maximum users, concurrent logins, and so on. Think of these as account restrictions.

- **Auth**: This is used to establish who the user is, most often, by prompting for a password. This module can also be used to grant group membership.

- **Password**: This type is used when updating a user's authentication token; again, most commonly, the password. Typically, one module will need to be loaded for each challenge and response authentication method.

- **Session**: This is associated with events that need to be complete before a user is given access to the server, such as creating a home directory, if required.

Control

The control field indicates the behavior of the PAM-API based on success or failure returned by the module.

- **required** (`success=ok new_authtok_reqd=ok ignore=ignore default=bad`): Failure will ultimately lead to the API returning `failure`, but only after the remaining modules have been invoked.

- **requisite** (`success=ok new_authtok_reqd=ok ignore=ignore default=die`): Like required, except control and failure is immediately returned to the calling service.

- **sufficient** (`success=done new_authtok_reqd=done default=ignore`): Success of a module with this type is enough to satisfy the authentication requirements unless a previously required module has failed. A failure of a module of this type is not fatal.

- **optional** (`success=ok new_authtok_reqd=ok default=ignore`): Success or failure of this module is not important.

 Recently, the second notation (within the brackets) is referred to for the control value, which is accepted to be a better explanation of the meaning.

The module path

The module path will consist of either the full filesystem path to the referenced module and the path would begin with the / filesystem or a relative to the `/lib/security` or `/lib64/security` directory.

Module arguments

The module arguments are a space delimited list of tokens that can modify the behavior of a module. The following is an example:

```
silent umask=077 skel=/etc/skel
```

We could put arguments together and use an example whereby we create a user's home directory for them on first login. This can be useful where we create many accounts in one go and do not want to overload the server creating the home directories at the same time. This is common for universities and so on where many accounts are created in batches.

Users would most probably connect to the server using SSH, so we should consider adding the following line to the `/etc/pam.d/sshd` file:

```
session  required  pam_mkhomedir.so  umask=0077 skel=/etc/skel
```

This mechanism utilizes PAM to create the home directory at user login.

Limits of PAM

Let's stick with using the SSH login at the moment. Many users will only access the server via SSH, perhaps using the PuTTY SSH client on Windows. If we want to control access to system resources, then we can implement restrictions using PAM and `pam_limits.so`. We should add the following line to the `/etc/pam.d/sshd` file:

```
session required pam_limits.so
```

This will implement the module, however, we still have to set the restrictions in the `/etc/security/limits.conf` file; the module reads from this file. The file's structure is set as follows with these elements making up a line in the limits file:

```
<domain> <type> <item> <value>
```

Domain

Domain represents to whom the limit is intended. This, most often, is a username such as `user1` or a group entry such as `@users`; the `@` symbol differentiates between user and group names. To implement a default restriction to apply to all accounts that do not have their own entry is the wildcard `*`.

Type

Type can be set to `soft`, `hard`, or both with `-`. Use the `hard` restriction for enforcing hard resource limits. These limits are set by the root user and enforced by the kernel. The user cannot raise their requirement of system resources above such values. Be cautious when enforcing restrictions before adequately testing, as it is possible to bring a system to a halt if enough processes cannot be spawned.

The `soft` restriction is used to enforce soft resource limits. These limits are the ones that the user can move up or down within the permitted range with any pre-existing hard limits. The values specified with this token can be thought of as default values for normal system usage. Use of the `-` symbol is to enforce both soft and hard resource limits together.

Item

The item represents the system resource on which the restriction is being made. Command items that can be restricted include the following:

- **nofile**: This sets the maximum number of open files
- **maxlogins**: This is the maximum number of logins for this user except for the user with uid=0
- **maxsyslogins**: This is the maximum number of all logins on a system
- **priority**: This is the priority to run user process with (negative values boost process priority)
- **nice**: This is the maximum nice priority allowed to raise to (Linux 2.6.12 and higher) values: [-20,19]

You can see from the preceding partial item list that it is possible to assign certain users a higher CPU priority than others, which is useful for call center groups whose access is more time sensitive than other accounts. The following example would give the telesales group a higher priority than standard users where the priority is normally 0:

```
*               -       priority    0
@telesales      -       priority    -5
```

It may also be useful to limit concurrent logins with an entry similar to the following:

```
@users   -    maxlogins   1
```

These limits might be very important to the running of your server and its security. So do take the time to investigate what is best in your environment, and more information can be found by referencing the manual page:

```
$ man 5 limits.conf
```

SELinux

I am not really sure if I can quantify how many blogs I read on the Internet where "the solution" to an issue is to disable SELinux, or at least set it into permissive mode. While I do not disagree that the immediate problem may then be resolved, it is a little like setting the filesystem permissions to rwx for all users authenticated or otherwise. Similarly, we all joke about users sticking post-it notes with password to the screen; there is little difference in this to an administrator disabling SELinux inappropriately.

There are reasons that the **mandatory access control (MAC)** list exists, and we as administrators should use it to our advantage. Traditionally, we are accustomed to using **discretionary access control (DAC)** lists and these can be set by users as well as root. The MAC is said to be mandatory, as it can only be applied and revoked by root.

First the DAC list is applied, and then the MAC list. SELinux never gives additional rights that were not there in the first place. The real advantage that we have is that we can give the same process different rights depending on the SELinux context in which it was started or is accessing. So, a process started as a service through the init daemon can have different rights to the same process that was started outside of the normal init process by a user. SELinux is very powerful, and we just need to understand how we can channel its power.

Reading the current SELinux mode

SELinux has two modes, but it can operate in three if you include the disabled mode. The operational modes are as follows:

- Enforcing
- Permissive

SELinux is enabled in both these modes, but only the `Enforcing` mode will apply and enforce SELinux policies. In `Permissive` mode, the policies are read but not acted upon; however, we can view any denials from the audit log. The log entries still appear as denials even though the denials are not enforced while in the `Permissive` mode. The `/usr/sbin/getenforce` command can be used to display the current SELinux mode:

```
$ getenforce
```

This setting can also be read from the `/selinux/enforce` file:

```
$ cat  /selinux/enforce
```

The integers 1 and 0 represent the SELinux modes: `Enforcing` and `Permissive` respectively. Note that the `/selinux` directory is the SELinux mountpoint in CentOS; in other systems, this may be `/sys/fs/selinux`, or you can check the output of `sestatus`, which is shown in the following screenshot:

```
[user@ldap1 pam.d]$ sestatus
SELinux status:                 enabled
SELinuxfs mount:                /selinux
Current mode:                   permissive
Mode from config file:          permissive
Policy version:                 24
Policy from config file:        targeted
[user@ldap1 pam.d]$ █
```

The mode can also be read from the `sestatus` (`/usr/bin/sestatus`) command; this command returns a little more information including the current mode as well as the mode configured in `/etc/selinux/config`.

Setting the SELinux mode

As with most tasks in Linux, setting the SELinux mode is very flexible, in that, it can be set in many ways. Firstly we will look at the use of `setenforce` (`/usr/sbin/setenforce`):

```
# setenforce 1
# setenforce Enforcing
# setenforce 0
# setenforce Permissive
```

The first two options are used to set the mode to `Enforcing` and the bottom two, to `Permissive`, either method can be used, as the word and integer have the same meaning as the `setenforce` command.

We can also set the mode by writing directly to the control file within the SELinux mountpoint:

```
# echo 1 > /selinux/enforce
# echo 0 > /selinux/enforce
```

If we need more ways to set this, we can also use kernel options at boot time. Appending to the kernel entry in the GRUB configuration file will have the effect of overwriting the default mode in the `/etc/selinux/config` file:

```
enforcing=1
enforcing=0
```

Lastly, we can configure the mode in the `/etc/selinux/config` file.

Preventing mode changes from the command line

I know many system administrators who will readily set the system to `Permissive` in order to provide a *quick fix*; if this is contrary to your administration policy, then you can enforce the mode at boot time by using the `setsebool` (`/usr/sbin/setsebool`) command; perhaps, as a script at system boot:

```
# setsebool secure_mode_policyload on
```

Once set, the mode cannot be changed from what was set during the startup process either from the file or boot parameters to the kernel. This can be seen from the following screenshot when the mode is attempted to be changed.

```
[root@localhost ~]# getenforce
Enforcing
[root@localhost ~]# setenforce 0
setenforce:  setenforce() failed
[root@localhost ~]#
```

The setting made in this way will persist until the next boot. If we would prefer this setting to always be in place, then we can make it truly persistent with the -P option. Do take care while using this, as it does what it says on the tin. The setting is then persisted.

Caution is advised in implementing the following command:
`# setsebool -P secure_mode_policyload on`

Understanding SELinux contexts

SELinux will try to match the context of the process to the context of the resource being accessed; the SELinux policy in effect will specify what access is allowed to the resource from a given context. A SELinux context consists of four fields, note that the user is a SELinux user as opposed to a standard Linux user:

- User
- Role
- Type
- Sensitivity

 Technically, a file has a type and a user or process a domain, but in reality both the type and the domain are suffixed with -t.

We can view the context of a file with `ls -Z` as follows:

`$ ls -Z /etc/hosts`

See the following screenshot:

```
[root@ldap1 ~]# ls -Z /etc/hosts
-rw-r--r--. root root system_u:object_r:net_conf_t:s0  /etc/hosts
[root@ldap1 ~]#
```

The output shows the SELinux user, role, type, and sensitivity for the `/etc/hosts` file:

- `system_u`
- `object_r`
- `net_conf_t`
- `s0`

We can view the SELinux context of a user with the command ID:

`$ id -Z`

See the following screenshot:

```
[user@ldap1 pam.d]$ id -Z
unconfined_u:unconfined_r:unconfined_t:s0-s0:c0.c1023
[user@ldap1 pam.d]$ █
```

We can see from the output of the command that the SELinux context for this user (user) is currently:

- unconfined_u
- unconfined_r
- unconfined_t
- s0 sensitivity (s0 starts and stops at s0) and any category (c0 through to c1023)

To view the SELinux context of a process, we can use the ps command. In this example, the process ID of 1629 represents the Nginx server:

 # ps -Z 1629

Well over 90 percent of SELinux policies work with the type (_t), so most often this is where we will be troubleshooting.

Troubleshooting SELinux

We will now look at what happens when the context of a file resource and process does not match the SELinux policy.

For the purpose of the demonstration, I will use CentOS 6.5 and the Apache httpd web server. To create a command SELinux issue the web server will be configured to access an aliased directory outside of the normal /var/www structure. This could mimic a typical process where you want to supply kickstart files via HTTP to aid the automatic installation of your workstations and servers.

Of course as soon as we work outside of the /var/www/ directory, the file context or labels will not match the expectation of the web server and access will be denied even though we meet the requirements of the DAC (file permissions).

 The web server configuration is correct to allow the URL /ks to point to /install/ks as this has been added in by way of an alias.

Consider the following commands:

```
# mkdir  -m 755 -p /install/ks
# cp /root/anaconda-ks.cfg /install/ks
# chmod 644 /install/ks/anaconda-ks.cfg
```

With this in place, we can restart the web server and test access to the normal web root and to the URL /ks. For ease of demonstration, I have installed the command-line browser w3m:

```
$ w3m localhost
```

This works and displays the standard welcome page. Now use the following command:

```
$ w3m localhost/ks
```

We will see a rather ominous **Forbidden** page, as shown in the following screenshot:

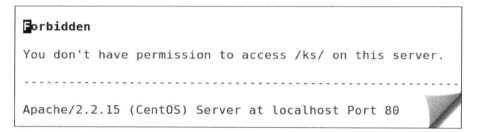

```
Forbidden

You don't have permission to access /ks/ on this server.

- - - - - - - - - - - - - - - - - - - - - - - - - - - - - - - - - - - - - - - - - -

Apache/2.2.15 (CentOS) Server at localhost Port 80
```

If we have the audit running, then SELinux denials are written to the audit log file, which is /var/log/audit/audit.log. We can use ausearch (available at /sbin/ausearch) to query this file:

```
# ausearch -m avc -ts recent
```

The options that we have used with the command are explained as follows:

- -m: This is the message to search for. We look for avc, which is the SELinux denials.

- -ts: This is the time start. If we use recent, it means from 10 minutes ago. The input today can also be commonly used.

The output of the `ausearch` command is shown in the following screenshot:

```
time->Sat Feb  1 18:05:51 2014
type=SYSCALL msg=audit(1391277951.222:266): arch=c000003e syscall=2 success=no exit=-
13 a0=7f604d213e88 a1=90800 a2=7f604d212298 a3=7f604d210928 items=0 ppid=1720 pid=173
1 auid=4294967295 uid=48 gid=48 euid=48 suid=48 fsuid=48 egid=48 sgid=48 fsgid=48 tty
=(none) ses=4294967295 comm="httpd" exe="/usr/sbin/httpd" subj=system_u:system_r:http
d_t:s0 key=(null)
type=AVC msg=audit(1391277951.222:266): avc:  denied  { read } for  pid=1731 comm="ht
tpd" name="ks" dev=sda3 ino=22341 scontext=system_u:system_r:httpd_t:s0 tcontext=unco
nfined_u:object_r:default_t:s0 tclass=dir
```

As we can see from the output, we have been denied read access for the PID of `1731`. We were running the `httpd` command while accessing the `/ks` directory, which is the inode `22341` in the filesystem of `sda3`. I am already impressed with this detail! The subject context has the type `httpd_t`, and the target has the type `default_t`. The subject is process 1731, and the target is the file in this case, and they do not match contexts, and access is denied.

We can use the command, `chcon` (available at `/usr/bin/chcon`), to change the SELinux context of the target either directly or by referencing the context of a directory that we know works, `/var/www/html`:

 # chcon -Rv --reference /var/www/html /install/ks

- `-v`: This makes the file verbose
- `-R`: This recurses all file and subdirectories
- `--reference`: This means copy the context from this file

Alternatively, we can set the context directly; although for accuracy and simplicity, I would prefer to use the `--reference` method:

 # chcon -Rv --type httpd_sys_content_t /install.ks

A process of type `httpd_t` can access resources that include `httpd_sys_content_t`, so with this simple change, we should now have access to the `/ks` directory through the web server without disabling SELinux.

Hardening Linux

We can really look at the previous example using SELinux to determine what we mean by hardening Linux, but this is often not the simple option. In the case of SELinux, the simple option is to set the `Permissive` mode but this does not go hand in hand with the best security for our systems.

Start with passwords and ask yourself how often are passwords changed on your system? When was the root password last changed? How many people have access to the root password? I come across many instances where the root password is never changed, and all administrators seem to have access to the root password. This is not a secure way of running your system even though it may help in the short term. Think of how many people who no longer work for your company have access to the root user password.

Of course, the system security has to work for you and the company, but the needs of a secure system should never be undervalued. For root access, consider using `sudo` instead of `su` and don't give the root password to each administrator.

Similarly, ensure strong password for accounts that have `sudo` rights as well as the root account.

Password auditing

I will use the term password auditing, as I do feel the tool highlights the need for adequate monitoring of password policies. You may well ask users to use strong passwords and to a degree we can enforce this use PAM modules. However, how many users have the same password, perhaps managers whose passwords are set by an assistant. It may also be the case that you have not realized how important it is not to allow weak passwords, often to save issues with forgetful users. The package john from Openwall (`http://www.openwall.com`) is one not to be missed to help you understand the need for strong passwords and algorithms.

The RPM is not in the repository but can be obtained from the Openwall site.

Preparing a password file

The password auditing tool john will be expecting users and passwords in one file, so we will use the `pwunconv` (`/usr/sbin/pwunconv`) command to add the passwords from the `/etc/shadow` file to the `/etc/passwd` file. Although this is not ideal, you have the password file; you can copy it to you own directory and use `pwconv` to switch back to the `/etc/shadow` file. The purpose of john is to show what is possible if password security isn't as it should be, and gaining rogue root privileges to the server is not unheard of. Even if john is run as a demonstration, it becomes a great tool to show what is possible with weak passwords, and a lab machine is fine for the demo.

The `pwunconv` command run as root is enough to read passwords from the shadow file into the `/etc/passwd` file.

Cracking passwords

Now that we have the prepared password file, we can copy it our own home directory:

```
# cp /etc/passwd /root/passwd
```

This step is not strictly required, but will allow you to convert back to shadow files as quickly as possible if this is not a lab machine. Run the following `john` command with the path through to the password file you would like to crack. The password file should contain users and passwords.

```
# john /root/passwd
```

This will then start cracking the passwords that it finds. In my file, there is only one user with a password, and it uses the default SHA512 encryption.

On my system, a simple password `Password1` took just 1 minute and 45 seconds to crack.

Weakening the algorithm

The password is weak enough, but what if we weakened the algorithm too? MD5 is only 128-bit or 16-byte encryption; what effect would that have on the result? We can use the `chpasswd` (available at `/usr/sbin/chpasswd`) command to generate passwords with MD5 rather than SHA512 encryption:

```
# echo andrew:Password | chpasswd  -c MD5
```

This command writes to the `/etc/passwd` file; if you need to write to your own file, send the output to `stdout` with `-s` and add the displayed text to your own password file:

```
# echo andrew:Password | chpasswd -S  -c MD5
```

We can now try running john again. However, to ensure that the new password is cracked fairly, delete the `john.pot` file that will contain the original password:

```
# rm ~/.john/john.pot
```

The `john.pot` file contains previously cracked passwords; so to run a true comparison, we should ensure that this file does not exist. Now, running the same test on my system, the crack, with the same password set but only with 128-bit encryption, took just 0.8 seconds.

Hardening the password

With a more secure password set, we can see the difference in time needed to crack the password, as a brute force attack will be needed. In this example, we use a password 27csg0TNWoUS. This is more of a passphrase to me, as I would remember this as *the 27th scout group of the Northwestern United States*. Anyway, I am sure you have your own ways to memorize complex passwords that don't involve post-it notes.

With this password set and MD5 encryption, I left the program running for 20 minutes, and it had not cracked the password. In time, moving from 0.8 seconds with a simple password to 20 minutes is a great demonstration on the use of secure passwords and how much more effective a strong password is compared to relying on a strong algorithm.

Start with these few steps, and your Linux system will be more secure from the outset.

Summary

In this chapter, we walked on the secure side of the road. Starting out with understanding a little of how PAM modules work and looking at ways in which we can use these modules to help us in administration and security. We saw that we could create user home directories, as they log in using PAM and a just-in-time method. We also looked at how we can restrict access and grant more access to users and groups using /etc/security/limits.conf. We then spent a little time to understand SELinux and securing our CentOS host.

The next chapter will discuss some general best practices guides to some of the elements that the book has taken us through.

11
Graduation Day

We have reached the last chapter of *CentOS System Administration Essentials*, and you are nearly a Linux Ninja; however, before you can pass with flying colors, you will learn some best practices in the deployment of CentOS Linux. This chapter will cover the subjects that we have specifically looked at and some other more generic CentOS best practices to consider when administering your systems. Additionally, we will take a quick peek at the new features that you will find in Enterprise Linux 7 from Red Hat and CentOS.

- **Securing remote access to your system**: Here, we take a look at OpenSSH and some considerations that you may want to review

- **OpenLDAP best practices**: Here, we ensure that your directory service is kept running the way that you want

- **Nginx best practices**: A quick guide to some dos and don'ts when configuring the web server

- **Mastering Puppet**: A checklist on what and how to secure on your Linux server.

- **What's new in CentOS 7**: This guide is predominately aimed at CentOS 6.5, but Enterprise Linux 7 is now available for both Red Hat and CentOS, and we will take a quick look at the highlights

Securing remote access to your system

Using **Secure Shell (SSH)** is a command method to gain remote access to your server. The security is implemented at one level using data encryption, but is augmented by server authentication, by default. Clients can compare the public key presented by the server against a list of trusted hosts, or as SSH names them, `known_hosts`. This is a little like using your web browser to visit HTTPS sites; occasionally, we may get warnings saying that the remote host is not trusted or cannot be identified. With SSH, instead of the browser holding the public key of the server, we have the `~/.ssh/known_hosts` file to store the SSH public key of hosts we connect to.

The SSH public key

The default behavior of the SSH client on CentOS and most Linux distributions is to prompt the user to accept the remote host's public SSH key when they first connect to that host. Unless the key is already present and perhaps preshared, on acceptance, the public key from the remote SSH host will be stored in the SSH client store for that user. Any subsequent times that the same user connects to the same remote host, the client will connect without the prompt as the host is already trusted.

Analyzing the risks of default settings

The default settings provide for a convenient, and mostly secure, mechanism in which we can obtain the public keys of remote hosts. Potentially, we have an issue where the remote host we connect to in the first instance is not the trusted host that we wish to connect to. As there is no authentication mechanism in place, we have to rely on trust and probability that in the first instance, the connection will be made to the correct host and not an imposter.

To work more securely, we can adjust the client settings so that it may only connect to hosts that are already trusted or, in other words, have their public key stored in the local keystore. To make this adjustment, we will need to edit the `/etc/ssh/ssh_config` file. The `StrictHostKeyChecking` directive is set to `ask` by default and should be edited to read `yes` to ensure we only connect when we have a preshared key.

Populating the keystore

If we choose the latter method where we wish the key to be already preshared, we need to address the method of populating the keystore. We can copy the server's public key to the client store manually or more easily, using the ssh-keyscan command. The command, although convenient, carries the same risks that are inherent to the client prompting to accept the key. If there is a malicious server during the scan, we will store the incorrect key. The reality is that the only secure method is sending a physical copy of the key to the client. Being able to centralize the client keystore would certainly make life much easier, and this can be achieved using the /etc/ssh/ssh_known_hosts file. This then does allow much easier manual population, as we only need the one client file rather than one per user on the client machine.

Public key authentication

Potentially, user passwords pose another security risk to your SSH servers. Although the password is encrypted over the wire, users, yes, we all know and love them, do share passwords, and perhaps use simple passwords when they should not. The settings for this are which authentication types are allowed are controlled on the server using the /etc/ssh/sshd.conf file. We can disable password-based authentication so that users have to use client keys. To disable passwords being used by our users for authentication, you will need to edit this file on the remote host; look for the PasswordAuthentication directive and ensure that it is set to no; the setting for PubKeyAuthentication should be set to yes.

With this in place, users will need to generate their own public and private key pairs on their client devices, using the ssh-keygen command. Their public keys should be copied to the ~/.ssh/authorized_keys file on the server; this can be achieved using the ssh-copy-id command:

```
ssh-copy-i <idfile>  user@server
```

Root logins

Root logins to an SSH server should never be allowed; I do not feel this is debatable at all on a production server. Users who need to administer the device can log in as a standard user and use sudo or su to gain privileges. This again is a controller in the /etc/ssh/sshd.conf file and the PermitRootLogin directive.

Conclusion

SSH provides a secure encryption mechanism to maintain data security across the network. Implementing `StrictHostKeyChecking` on the client will also allow for host authentication so we can be sure that we are sending our secure information to the correct server. To enhance client authentication, disable root logins to the server and allow only authentication from clients with preshared user keys.

Best practices of OpenLDAP

We have seen during the course of this book that we can centralize user accounts on an OpenLDAP server or, if we want to ease some administration features on CentOS, we can use the 389-ds. Either way, the underlying directory is OpenLDAP. Now, of course, if the user accounts exits from the directory, then so do our authentication tokens (passwords). We need to ensure that this is secure and effective. OpenLDAP supports different mechanisms for authentication; each, of course, has advantages and disadvantages as follows:

- **Simple bind**: Using the simple bind authentication mechanism, clients pass a clear text password to authenticate themselves to the server. This carries three potential threats: the password can be collected from a network capture, the password can be collected by a host spoofing the server's address, and the password can be obtained through a malicious attack on the server. Using LDAPS will protect against the first two threats, but not the third. It is best to avoid simple bind authentication, if possible.

- **Simple Authentication and Security Layer (SASL) external**: This allows the use of external authentication such as client X.509 certificates (TLS public keys) to authenticate users, and can overcome inherent password issues. If the LDAP client and LDAP server are on the same machine, it is also possible to use the **LDAP over IPC (LDAPI)** method of the SASL authentication, where the Linux credentials of the user are used to access the directory.

- **SASL passwords**: It is possible to use password-based authentication with SASL, but the threats then are similar to simple bind.

If you use password-based authentication, it is often thought prudent to implement a lockout of accounts after so many failed attempts. Although this is possible in an OpenLDAP password policy, the reality is that password attacks are often more subtle than this in today's environment, and all this provides a mechanism for attackers to lock accounts.

It is also becoming more common to allow users to reset their own password if they do not remember it. Although this does alleviate a load from the help desk, it is often a weak leak in your security chain as the challenge response questions often proffered are too easily known or guessed by potential attackers.

In any directory system, there is a schema that describes each object that can be created, such as a user or group, and the attributes are properties that can exist for that object. Although it is possible to edit the schema for any given object or attribute, it is best to create your own definitions if additional attributes are required for an object rather than add them directory to the existing schema. In the long run, altering existing objects can cause issues with replication to other servers if the schema is not identical on all servers.

Best practices of Nginx

If you choose to implement the Nginx web server, there are few things that we should take a look at to endure the longevity of your web service.

From a security perspective, your web server could be accessible to the whole world, everyone. For this reason, we should ensure that some basic security threats are protected:

- **SELinux**: Ensure that we have set SELinux to `Enforcing` on our CentOS system that hosts Nginx.

- **DocumentRoot**: Mount the DocumentRoot structure independently as its own filesystem, ensuring that malicious writes will not crash the Linux host if the disk fills, and secondly the partition or disk can be mounted with minimal rights, for example, `LABEL=web /var/www ext4 ro,nosuid,noexec,nodev,noatime 0 2`.

- **Use a host-based firewall**: Allow only incoming TCP ports 80 and 443. Often, only outgoing UDP port 123 along with outgoing dynamic TCP ports need to be open, with port 123 being for time synchronization.

- **Restrict HTTP methods available to Nginx.** The RFC 2616 allows many HTTP access methods; most will not be needed on your server. We can add code similar to the following to check for matches that are not equal to GET, HEAD, and POST. The code will then disallow other access methods that we do not require, such as DELETE, SEARCH, and others:

```
if ( $request_method !~ ^(GET|POST|HEAD)$ ) {
    return 403;
}
```

- **User Agents**: We may also choose to block certain user agents, browsers that are often associated with scanners, bots, or spammers. The `$httpd_user_agent` variable in an HTTP header will show what the browser is, for example Internet Explorer, Mozilla, and so on. Other than these normal browsers, there are also automated browsers that can access your site through scripts such as `wget` and `BBBike`. Try adding this to your `nginx.conf` file to prevent these agents:

```
if ($http_user_agent ~* wget|BBBike|LWP::Simple ) {
    return 403;
}
```

- **Limit access by IP**: If a particular directory should only be accessible to the internal network, then you can use code similar to this in your host configuration:

```
location /var/www/docs {
    allow 192.168.0.0/24
    deny all
}
```

- **Limit file ownership**: The Nginx web server will run as a named user, `nginx`. The temptation is to add the Nginx user as the owner of the DocumentRoot directory and all web content therein. This is ill advised as the document owner, user, or group can gain additional privileges such as deleting a document that you cannot write to. Typically, the `nginx` user should gain access via `others`, and we limited `others` to `r-x` on directories and `r--` on files. Typical file permissions should be similar to the following:

```
-rw-r--r-- 1 root root 1000 Feb 1 10:00 index.html
```

Mastering Puppet

When using the Puppet server to manage your configuration centrally, it is worth remembering a few pertinent facts in the setup of the Puppet master.

- **Use modules**: The `/etc/puppet/modules` directory allows the creation of modules. Modules are subdirectories created within the Puppet `ModulePath` directive, and contains files and configurations that need to be distributed to the client as part of its desired state. This simplifies the Puppet configuration, as related files are all within the module directory.

- **Use version control**: Puppet itself does not have version control, but we can use something like GIT or **subversion (svn)** to maintain the previous copies of configurations.

- **Style**: When writing Puppet configuration, standardizing the syntax style helps in maintenance and readability. The Puppet Labs style guide can be found at `http://docs.puppetlabs.com/guides/style_guide.html`.

What's new in CentOS 7

CentOS 7 was released in June 2014, along with the earlier release of Red Hat Enterprise Linux 7. Along with the introduction of the Linux kernel 3.10 in this release, there are other significant updates to the distribution.

Locale

The system locale information can be conveniently set and displayed using the `localectl` command:

```
$ localectl status
```

The output can be seen in the following screenshot:

```
[andrew@centos7 Desktop]$ localectl status
   System Locale: LANG=en_GB.UTF-8
       VC Keymap: uk
      X11 Layout: gb
[andrew@centos7 Desktop]$
```

Time and date information

Similar to the locale information, CentOS 7 includes a simple command to display and manage time and date settings on the host system: `/usr/bin/timedatectl`. This really is a godsend to us as administrators; even if we only use the command to display the output, this one command will display the time, timezone, and NTP settings. Take a look at the output of the `timedatectl` command without options in the following screenshot:

```
[andrew@centos7 Desktop]$ timedatectl
      Local time: Sat 2014-07-19 20:26:30 BST
  Universal time: Sat 2014-07-19 19:26:30 UTC
        Timezone: Europe/London (BST, +0100)
     NTP enabled: yes
NTP synchronized: yes
 RTC in local TZ: no
      DST active: yes
 Last DST change: DST began at
                  Sun 2014-03-30 00:59:59 GMT
                  Sun 2014-03-30 02:00:00 BST
 Next DST change: DST ends (the clock jumps one hour backwards) at
                  Sun 2014-10-26 01:59:59 BST
                  Sun 2014-10-26 01:00:00 GMT
[andrew@centos7 Desktop]$ 
```

Staying with the `timedatectl` command, we can change the date using the following command:

```
# timedatectl set-time 2014-07-19
```

The time can be set using the same option with time as the argument, shown as follows:

```
# timedatectl set-time 23:02:23
```

NTP time synchronization can be enabled and disabled with the following command; though, it uses the news system service manager to enable and disable the time service:

```
# timedatectl set-ntp yes
```

This is really a Swiss Army knife of a command; you will get to learn very quickly.

Managing services

`Systemd` is now the system and service manager in CentOS 7 and replaces Upstart as the default init system. This not only replaces Upstart, but is backwards compatible with the traditional System V init scripts. For us as administrators, the main command to become familiar with is `/usr/bin/systemctl`.

Starting with the `status` subcommand, we can immediately see how `systemctl` works well for us. Here, we look at the status of the SSH service:

```
# systemctl status sshd
```

The output is quite extensive and includes the **Process ID (PID)** and recent logfile activity. You can view this in the following screenshot.

```
[root@centos7 ~]# systemctl status sshd
sshd.service - OpenSSH server daemon
   Loaded: loaded (/usr/lib/systemd/system/sshd.service; enabled)
   Active: active (running) since Sat 2014-07-19 19:13:17 BST; 2h 1min ago
  Process: 1089 ExecStartPre=/usr/sbin/sshd-keygen (code=exited, status=0/SUCCES
S)
 Main PID: 1123 (sshd)
   CGroup: /system.slice/sshd.service
           └─1123 /usr/sbin/sshd -D

Jul 19 19:13:17 centos7.tup.com systemd[1]: Started OpenSSH server daemon.
Jul 19 19:13:18 centos7.tup.com sshd[1123]: Server listening on 0.0.0.0 port 22.
Jul 19 19:13:18 centos7.tup.com sshd[1123]: Server listening on :: port 22.
Hint: Some lines were ellipsized, use -l to show in full.
[root@centos7 ~]# 
```

We can stop the service using the following command:

```
# systemctl stop sshd
```

To disable the autostart of the service, we will use the `disable` subcommand:

```
# systemctl disable sshd
```

A service that is disabled can still be started by the administrator; the term disabled just means that the autostart of the service is disabled. A new feature that `systemd` brings is the ability to prevent a service from being started manually:

```
# systemctl mask sshd
```

Even if an administrator tried to start the service while it is masked, the service will not start. If it is required to re-enable the service, then an administrator would need to use the `unmask` subcommand:

```
# systemctl unmask sshd
```

Additional ways to repair your machine than just using the single user mode

In traditional environments, we are perhaps used to using run level 1, or the single mode, as the mechanism to place the system into the maintenance mode. The concept of run levels has changed with system, and we now have targets rather than run levels. To place a running system in maintenance, we can use the following command:

```
# systemctl rescue
```

You will be prompted for the root user password to complete the operation. If this still does not allow you to repair your system, then there is an emergency target that starts even fewer services, again allowing only root access:

```
# systemctl emergency
```

The emergency target is much more similar to starting a CentOS 6.5 machine with the kernel argument `init=/bin/bash`. You may also have guessed from some of these commands that we can also power off and reboot systems with `systemctl`:

```
# systemctl reboot
```

```
# systemctl halt
```

Of course, the `shutdown` command is still here and can be used for this purpose too.

Remote management

The management of remote systems is possible with system too, which also uses the same `systemctl` command. If we need to see the status of the `atd` service on the host `s1.tup.com`, we can issue the following command:

```
$ systemctl -H root@s1.tup.com status atd
```

This simply makes use of an SSH connection to the remote host, so port 22 and SSHD must be accessible on the remote host that we monitor.

Systemd and nonstandard subcommands

The subcommands that are available from `systemctl` through `systemd` are now standardized, whereas with System V init scripts, it was possible to have any argument or subcommands added to the script. For example, with the Apache HTTPD service in CentOS 6.5, we could issue the `service httpd graceful` command. The `graceful` argument is unique to the web server, so it is not built as a subcommand within `systemctl`; however, the same result can be achieved through the use of the `apachectl graceful` command. While on the subject of the Apache web server, the default DocumentRoot has changed from `/var/www` to `/usr/share/httpd`.

The Samba 4.1 package

For the Windows domain, file, and print services, Samba 4.1 replaces the aged Samba 3, which was supplied with CentOS 6.5 and earlier systems.

Filesystem changes

The default filesystem is now XFS, replacing ext4. XFS has been around for a long time, but is obviously catching the attention of the Enterprise Linux community now.

Password policies

The PAM module that enforces password quality now defaults to `pam_pwquality`, replacing the older `pam_cracklib`. Editing the `/etc/security/pwquality.conf` file will allow you to specify the minimum password length and password complexity. The password complexity consists of:

- **minclass**: This is the minimum number of character class types, uppercase, lowercase, numeric, and non-alphanumeric
- **maxsequence**: This limits the number of consecutive characters of the same class, such as `12345` or `bcfag`; both have a sequence of five characters, whereas `bcafG` only has a sequence of four characters from the same class (lowercase)
- **maxrepeat**: This limits the number of repeating characters

The existing file can act as an example, or we can use the manual using the `man 5 pwqulality.conf` command for more detailed information.

Summary

You are now ready to walk out into the world and declare your new-found knowledge of CentOS. I have been able to help you through some simple best practice goals to manage the services we looked at throughout this book as well as introduce some new elements of CentOS 7. Of course, for a long time, you will still come across plenty of CentOS 6 systems to keep you busy, and most elements are consistent from Version 6 to Version 7, but keeping up to date with the latest enhancements is always useful.

Index

Thank you for buying
CentOS System Administration Essentials

About Packt Publishing

Packt, pronounced 'packed', published its first book "*Mastering phpMyAdmin for Effective MySQL Management*" in April 2004 and subsequently continued to specialize in publishing highly focused books on specific technologies and solutions.

Our books and publications share the experiences of your fellow IT professionals in adapting and customizing today's systems, applications, and frameworks. Our solution based books give you the knowledge and power to customize the software and technologies you're using to get the job done. Packt books are more specific and less general than the IT books you have seen in the past. Our unique business model allows us to bring you more focused information, giving you more of what you need to know, and less of what you don't.

Packt is a modern, yet unique publishing company, which focuses on producing quality, cutting-edge books for communities of developers, administrators, and newbies alike. For more information, please visit our website: www.packtpub.com.

About Packt Open Source

In 2010, Packt launched two new brands, Packt Open Source and Packt Enterprise, in order to continue its focus on specialization. This book is part of the Packt Open Source brand, home to books published on software built around Open Source licenses, and offering information to anybody from advanced developers to budding web designers. The Open Source brand also runs Packt's Open Source Royalty Scheme, by which Packt gives a royalty to each Open Source project about whose software a book is sold.

Writing for Packt

We welcome all inquiries from people who are interested in authoring. Book proposals should be sent to author@packtpub.com. If your book idea is still at an early stage and you would like to discuss it first before writing a formal book proposal, contact us; one of our commissioning editors will get in touch with you.

We're not just looking for published authors; if you have strong technical skills but no writing experience, our experienced editors can help you develop a writing career, or simply get some additional reward for your expertise.

[PACKT] open source ✿
PUBLISHING   community experience distilled

CentOS 6 Linux Server Cookbook

ISBN: 978-1-84951-902-1   Paperback: 374 pages

A practical guide to installing, configuring, and administering the CentOS community-based enterprise server

1. Delivering comprehensive insight into the CentOS server with a series of starting points that show you how to build, configure, maintain, and deploy the latest edition of one of the world's most popular community-based enterprise servers.

2. Providing beginners and more experienced individuals alike with the opportunity to enhance their knowledge by delivering instant access to a library of recipes that addresses all aspects of the CentOS server and puts you in control.

Instant Ubuntu

ISBN: 978-1-78328-087-2   Paperback: 54 pages

Your complete guide to making the switch to Ubuntu

1. Learn something new in an Instant! A short, fast, focused guide delivering immediate results.

2. Focuses on making new users feel comfortable switching to Ubuntu.

3. Discover the top applications and features.

4. Learn everything you need to know to install, configure, and get started with using the Ubuntu desktop.

Please check **www.PacktPub.com** for information on our titles

Getting Started with Citrix XenApp 6.5

ISBN: 978-1-84968-666-2   Paperback: 478 pages

Design and implement Citrix farms based on XenApp 6.5

1. Use Citrix management tools to publish applications and resources on client devices with this book and eBook.

2. Deploy and optimize XenApp 6.5 on Citrix XenServer, VMware ESX, and Microsoft Hyper-V virtual machines and physical servers.

OpenStack Cloud Computing Cookbook
Second Edition

ISBN: 978-1-78216-758-7   Paperback: 396 pages

Over 100 recipes to successfully set up and manage your OpenStack cloud environments with complete coverage of Nova, Swift, Keystone, Glance, Horizon, Neutron, and Cinder

1. Updated for OpenStack Grizzly.

2. Learn how to install, configure, and manage all of the OpenStack core projects including new topics like block storage and software-defined networking.

3. Learn how to build your private cloud utilizing devops and continuous integration tools and techniques.

Please check **www.PacktPub.com** for information on our titles

56342856R00098

Made in the USA
Lexington, KY
20 October 2016